My Provincetown

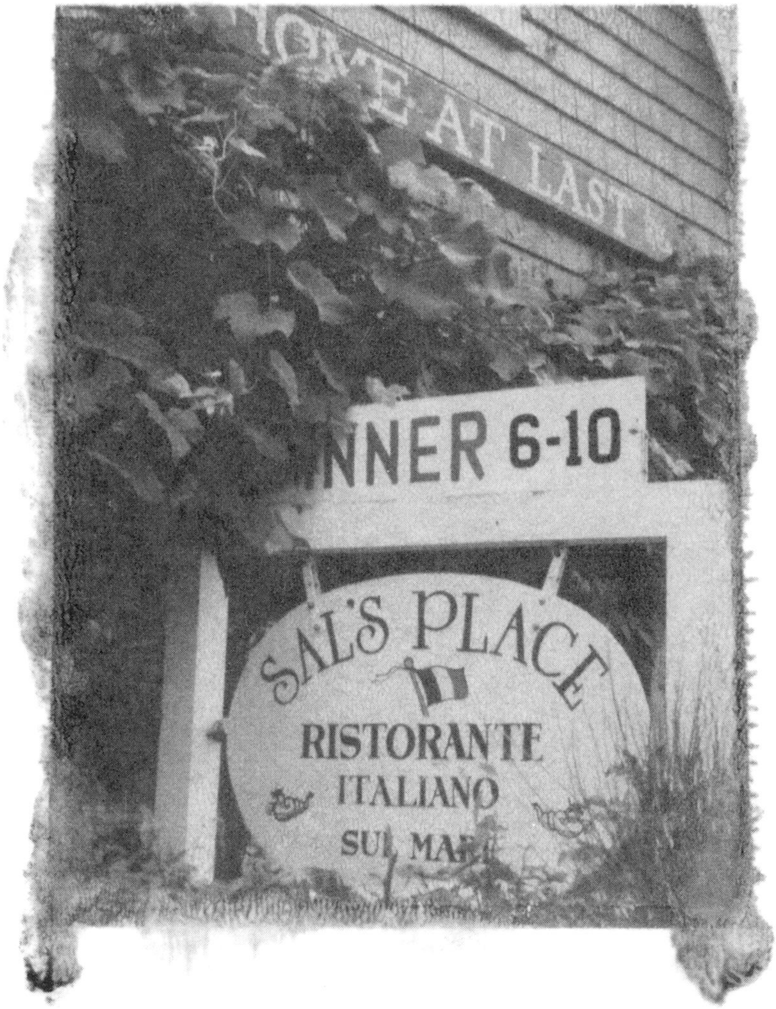
AT LAST
NNER 6-10
SAL'S PLACE
RISTORANTE
ITALIANO

My Provincetown

Memories of a
Cape Cod Childhood

AMY WHORF McGUIGGAN

COMMONWEALTH EDITIONS
BEVERLY • MASSACHUSETTS

Library of Congress Cataloging-in-Publication Data

McGuiggan, Amy Whorf, 1956–

    My Provincetown: memories of a Cape Cod childhood / Amy Whorf McGuiggan.

    p. cm.

ISBN 1-889833-55-X

1. McGuiggan, Amy Whorf, 1956 — Childhood and youth. 2. Provincetown (Mass.) — Biography. 3. Provincetown (Mass.) — Social life and customs — 20th century. 4. Cape Cod (Mass.) — Social life and customs — 20th century. I. Title.

    F74.P96 M38 2003

    974.4'92 — dc21   2002154256

Jacket design by Joyce C. Weston.

Interior design by Christopher Kuntze, CDK Design.

Photo on front of jacket from the collection of the author; Polaroid transfer process photos of A Home at Last (on frontispiece) and of the West End Racing Club (on page 166) by the author.

Printed in Canada.

Published by Commonwealth Editions,

an imprint of Memoirs Unlimited, Inc.,

266 Cabot Street, Beverly, Massachusetts 01915.

Visit our Web site: www.commonwealtheditions.com.

Contents

Acknowledgments

THIS BOOK EMERGED — like a sculpture from rough stone — with many gifted, sure hands doing the shaping and smoothing.

I owe my deepest gratitude to Webster Bull, who believed in this book from the beginning. Penny Stratton gave the book its personality. I learned as much about my story from her as I did from writing it. I owe thanks to copy-editor Margaret Eckman, proofreader Lida Stinchfield, and production specialist Jill Atkinson. Thanks, too, to Joyce Weston for her alluring jacket design, which truly represents my Provincetown, and to Christopher Kuntze for his elegant interior design.

And to Robert Finch, whose kindness will never be forgotten, a heartfelt thank-you.

For Professors Caryl Rivers and James Brann,
without whom I could not have
begun this story . . .

and for Danny, Ben, and Jake, without whom
I could not have finished it.

I remember my youth and the feeling that will never come back any more — the feeling that I could last for ever, outlast the sea, the earth, and all men. . . .

— Joseph Conrad, *Youth*

Getting There

ONCE A YEAR my father cooked us all breakfast. I don't remember him in the kitchen otherwise — unless, like many men of his generation, he was making a pest of himself, dipping into this, sampling that, shaving a slice off the roast, an edge off the pork chop.

But on that one morning each year he would pile a plate high with scrambled eggs, bacon, and a few slices of hastily buttered toast, fill a glass halfway with orange juice, and set the meal before us. There was a hash-house style to his work, the way he flipped and poured and delivered the meal, a touch of impatience that said more than words ever could.

To see my father actually cooking, rather than interfering with the cooking, could mean only one thing: it was the day we were leaving for Provincetown, for the start of summer vacation. That we were going to Provincetown was no secret. For weeks there had been anticipation. I knew we were going, but not *when*. There is no point in telling a kid, "We leave a week from Saturday." It means nothing; at least it didn't to me. I had no concept of time back then. Summer vacation in Provincetown became something tangible only when I saw my father wrestling with the bacon and eggs.

All year I would wait for this day, and I don't recall ever regretting that I was leaving my hometown, my friends, the neighborhood. None of those friends went away for the summer. A weekend, maybe, but not the summer. I was the only one who did, and in my mind, that made me special. My mother would save all year for this vacation, which required careful budgeting and considerable sacrifice. She was willing to put in that effort, though, for us and for herself. Provincetown — unconventional, tolerant, and creatively inspiring — was her respite from what she saw as the stifling conventions of suburban living.

If there were times in my social-climbing hometown that my clothes or my bike, my bedroom or my Barbie outfits did not measure up, I didn't care. I was wealthier than any of my neighbors because I had Provincetown. I had pleasures and enjoyments that no one could ever take away from me.

I uncoupled completely from everything and everyone when it came time to leave for P-Town, which was not the case when it came time to leave the Cape and return home at summer's end. Tucked in the back of the car that day in early summer, I'd already be thinking that I wouldn't want the summer to end, wouldn't want to leave for another year — a lifetime to me — the place that made me feel truly alive, the place where I felt in my marrow that I belonged. It was Provincetown that best defined who I was, not Hingham, where I lived nine months a year.

There had never been any discussion about going anywhere but Provincetown for summer vacation. No cottage on Lake Winnipesaukee with the aunts and cousins, no woodsy Maine hideaway. Certainly no trips abroad. Always Provincetown. My father had grown up in Provincetown after his parents relocated there during the Depression. My mother, originally from the Dorchester neighborhood of Boston, found Provincetown as an art student during the late 1940s. Though my grandfather John Whorf, a well-known painter, had died in 1959, my grandmother Vivienne still lived in town. My parents had longtime friends. My father was still known as Johnny. From my first days, I went to the town belonging.

✆ I loved watching clothes and groceries get stuffed into the bags and boxes that, in turn, got stuffed into the back and onto the top of our dingy white Falcon wagon. My mother would methodically check lists and rooms to be sure that nothing had been overlooked. How many times that morning would someone say, "Don't let the cat get out!" "Is the stove off?" "Are the windows upstairs shut?" "Is the cellar door locked?" "Are you forgetting anything?" "Where are the car keys?" My father would try to be helpful, or at least try to look as though he was being helpful, but ultimately he and we were in the way. With tension mounting, my mother would finally bark, "John, just take them outside and let me finish up here." Year after year this drama played out; the final act came when we hoisted our twelve-foot aluminum motorboat on top of the car, atop boxes and suitcases. We had that boat for years. It had a small outboard motor, a ten-horsepower Johnson, and a pair of oars. It was as unsteady in the water as a canoe, but it enhanced the experience of Provincetown immensely.

While my father double-checked the knots on the ropes that secured our little boat, we'd pile into the car, into our designated spots. My two younger brothers occupied most of the backseat, while I, in a small carved-out space in the back, would nestle among suitcases, the shaft of the outboard, and a cardboard box holding Frisky, the family calico cat — who, despite a tranquilizer from the vet, always suffered terribly during the two-hour journey.

When I was ready, it seemed an eternity before we'd actually get underway. Finally, we'd pull out of the driveway, my mother behind the wheel because my father had never learned to drive. Then came the inevitable discussion about whether the stove had, in fact, been turned off. To ease her mind, my mother would pull back into the driveway and go back into the house, returning reassured.

Leaving Hingham, our quiet suburban neighborhood south of Boston, I never looked back at our white house; my father's flower garden with the saucer-sized Oriental poppies already opening; the woods beyond the railroad tracks where we built our forts; the house of my best friend, Wendy, across the street; the old naval ammunition depot where we played every afternoon after school, exploring deteriorating World War II bunkers. My thoughts were already on arriving in Provincetown. I knew what this first day there would be like: I would help, reluctantly, with the unpacking, then change into my bathing suit, throw on an oversized T-shirt, and scramble across the street to call on the O'Donnell sisters, who would already have arrived for the summer from Worcester. We'd go for a swim, and we'd have a long conversation on the beach, all the while nestling into the coarse sand, letting the glassy white grains of quartz, the gray feldspar, the reddish garnet slip like liquid through my fingers and toes, getting reacquainted with its special mustiness, relishing having reconnected after so many months.

My brothers and I would pass the trip south on Route 3 squabbling, whacking each other, tossing things at one another, or, in more civilized moments, tallying the license plates of cars that passed us on their way to Cape Cod. Maybe some of these people were going to P-Town, too. I often wondered about that. How many were going where we were going? And if they weren't going to P-Town, why not? Why would they go anywhere else? If, at the end of our journey, I spotted a car that we had seen at the beginning, I would be thrilled, feeling a kinship with its passengers, thinking that simply by their presence in Provincetown I knew something intimate and essential about them.

We knew that highway cold, every bump, every incline, every decline. We'd cross over the sprawling salt marsh of the North River, then pass through Duxbury, Kingston, Plymouth. We knew when to fix our eyes outside, up ahead, just above the tree line. Who would be the first to see the superstructure of the Sagamore Bridge, an apparition on a horizon of scrub oak and pine?

On sunny days the bridge put on a dazzling laser show, shooting shafts of incandescent white from its superstructure. On overcast days the bridge's pewter tones were barely distinguishable from those of the gray sky. Under either condition, from afar, the bridge looked delicate, lacey. Closer, it would begin to loom, like that first terrifying ascent on a roller coaster. At the busy rotary that lay at the foot of the bridge where traffic could back up for miles on a summer day, we'd stop at Sorenti's — coffee for my parents, bathrooms for us — and then make our way down a small side street, down to the banks of the Cape Cod Canal. The view was usually ours alone, the turnoff unpaved, the banks sandy, precarious, and casual with wildflowers, bittersweet, and bayberry. Overhead, the Sagamore Bridge would stretch across the canal. From where we stood, its construction had the airiness and gentle rise and fall of an apple pie. We would stretch our legs, watch passing traffic — both vehicles on the bridge as well as boats in the canal — and eat a lunch of tuna fish or egg salad sandwiches. You'd think we had been on the road for hours. In fact, we were less than fifty miles from home. It seemed already like a long trip, and there were still fifty miles to go. How many times over the next hour would one of us ask, "Are we there yet?"

Around the rotary we'd go, then up, up, onto the bridge, across the canal. That man-made fissure, completed in 1914, eliminated for many vessels the long voyage around the outer shore of Cape Cod and across the treacherous shoaled water that had, over the decades, swallowed ships and more than deserved to be called the "graveyard of the Atlantic." I would always look up as we crossed, never down, terrified that at any moment we would slip from this tightrope and plunge to our deaths, look up at the steel girders that from a distance had looked like a child's erector set. As we drove under them, their thickness and weight, their enormous bolts and shafts and wire cable through and around which the wind swirled and rushed and bullied our car, showed themselves. We reached the pinnacle and began our descent.

We had left Route 3 behind, that umbilical cord that connected me to another world. Route 6 would now take us all the way to P-Town without interruption. I never remembered much of that leg of the journey, having been lulled by the time we reached Hyannis — a twenty-minute drive from the bridge — into thoughts of what was waiting at the journey's end, the journey never as interesting for me as was the destination. I would stir forty-five minutes later when the rich odor of the salt marsh in Wellfleet ambushed us as we came around the bend, stir where the Cape begins to open up, where the sky overpowers, the vegetation cowers, where the landscape begins to hint at the sensuous zing that waits at Provincetown. The end was near, I knew, when we passed the highway sign in Truro, the last town before Provincetown, that announced, "Provincetown, Either Way." It meant that you could choose Route 6A, the local road, frost-heaved and cracked, gray and puddled with sand, which snakes through Truro, up and down over the dunes and into Provincetown; or you could continue on Route 6, the four-lane state highway with smooth, oiled, black pavement that the summer days puddled with mirages, the quicker though no less scenic route into town. That road sign became something of a lower Cape landmark as well as an insider's pun, and anyone who knew the tolerance Provincetown had always shown toward homosexuality was privy to the pun. During my teen years there were T-shirts that were worn with humor by gays and straights alike. At some point, whether because of sexual politics or simply wear and tear, the sign was replaced with one that announced blandly "Shore Route," which I've never seen printed on a T-shirt.

Regardless of whether we turned left or stayed straight, we were so close that my heart was racing. God, couldn't my mother drive any faster? In the distance, the Pilgrim Monument appeared, thrusting above the densely settled, hunkered-down village. The monument, the cupola of the Chrysler Art Museum, the steeple of the Universalist Church, and the spire of Town Hall defined the horizon.

Pilgrim Lake, at one time open to the sea and known by locals as East Harbor, spread out on our right, settled in at the edge of magnificent parabolic dunes, tawny, unmarked except for a thin line of half-buried snow fencing running across the top that laced the dune to the sky. Skittish sands teased the shoulder of the black asphalt. *Rosa rugosa* and bayberry bloomed in the median. On our left, the harbor side, low rock jetties reached out perpendicularly from the beach at regular intervals. The waters might be light, lively, prancing up onto the sand. Or they might be moody and riled up, the bear claws scratching at the surface.

From the highway, I saw the grains from thousands of years past wrapped in a flat, narrow spiral around the harbor. Long Point, the thin, crooked finger of the sand spit, beckoned me to keep coming. We passed Snail Road. Howland Street. Conwell. We turned on to Shankpainter Road, then Bradford Street, then a left onto Franklin, which slid down into Commercial. At the bottom of the hill, at Kelly's Corner, also known as Lancey's Corner, was the cold-storage plant, four stories tall, noisy, tired, and weather-beaten. The intersection was jammed with pedestrians and bicycles. A few wizened Portuguese men sat on the bench at the bend and took in the procession. The multitude of commercial enterprises that congested the downtown tapered off here to a gallery or two and Bertie Perry's liquor store. As we crossed onto Commercial Street and rounded the bend, I got a nourishing peek between the houses of the harbor and the gangly Freeman's Wharf. Next to the houses, an open lot was a tangled thicket of wild raspberry vines, shiny poison ivy, and fragrant sand roses. Adjacent was Flyer's Boat Rental, nothing more than a tiny wheelhouse at the edge of a wooden deck set on short pilings driven into the beach. A couple of beach chairs encircled an old cable spool that had found a new life as a table. Into its center was set an oversized beach umbrella. Just yards offshore, Flyer's flotilla of orange-and-white wooden dories was scattered, some with tiny black outboards, others with a pair of oars resting in the locks, sweeping silently around on their moorings. All summer long visitors would find their way to Flyer's to rent a boat, to putter around the harbor, to drop a fishing line, to find that perspective that can be found only in a boat.

My mother would keep an eye open for a precious parking spot along the street. An inconspicuous sign announced Sal's Place, an Italian restaurant. A narrow alley separated the restaurant from a comely, two-story, red-stained shingled building, trimmed in white, its facade-covered with rambler rose and grapevines. Obscured by the luscious growth was a sign nailed to the front of the building. It was faded and peeling, but I could make out the words as easily as if they have been in flashing hot pink neon: "A Home at Last."

A Home at Last

MY PARENTS FIRST RENTED "A Home at Last" sometime in the mid-1960s, and the shorefront cottage became the center of my Provincetown experience. I have lived other places longer than I lived in that cottage, but the summers at A Home at Last were impressionable months from which I've retained more detail and memories than from my school days and my hometown neighborhood. I remember the smell of the bar soap in the kitchen, "Windy" and "Carrie-Anne" playing on my brother's transistor radio, the clunk of the refrigerator door closing, the encrusted frying pan that my father used to fry his mackerel.

All these years later, I can still remember precisely the layout of A Home at Last. We stayed upstairs, in two rooms. That five of us — not to mention the occasional friend or relative from home who came to visit — could coexist for weeks under such conditions was probably only possible because we had pared down our needs to the minimum and we were rarely inside. I never gave a thought to personal space or privacy and, in fact, always felt cozy and secure tucked in my cot at night, my brothers' beds across from and at the foot of mine. There was something about a contained space and being forced to keep it orderly, having my possessions close at hand, that was reassuring to me.

My parents, no doubt, thought differently about space and privacy, their physical and emotional health probably craving more of both. And although the two rooms were all we had, there was one saving grace — the deck outside our front door, a promontory overlooking openness.

By midday the unshaded deck sizzled under the Provincetown sun. We scampered across, singeing the bottoms of our feet and gradually building leathery soles. By summer's end they had toughened enough to withstand most anything.

The deck railings were draped all summer with bathing suits, bulky orange life jackets, and an assortment of wet towels, no two of which matched. The only permanent outdoor furniture were a faded wicker settee whose cushion was always wet and a cable spool table littered with coffee cups and wine glasses, binoculars, packs of Pall Malls, books of matches, and a clamshell ashtray spilling over with stubbed out butts, half of them rimmed with red lipstick. Behind the settee we stowed the collection of fishing rods and plastic tackle boxes. Purple petunias flourished in long planters that lined the perimeter of the deck.

Inside, the cottage was airy, unfinished, the ceiling with exposed beams, the walls whitewashed with exposed studs. A tiny gas stove sat to the left of the front door and next to it, the icebox, round-edged and resembling an old-style radio. Tucked into the corner under the roof peak was the sink, soapstone, I think. The white-speckled, gray-blue bare floor coughed up the sand of summers past and collected our contribution in its interstices. Over the course of the summer, the walls became a gallery where my mother thumbtacked her impressionistic watercolors of the world outside our front door. There they would hang for a few days, maybe a week, subjected to the most demanding scrutiny — hers. It mattered little if everyone who visited praised the half-sheets. If my mother found something, anything, wanting with the color or the composition, down the painting came and another sunny-day attempt would be made on the reverse. I always knew which ones she was partial to. They were slipped into frames and mats and were still hanging as the last days of vacation approached.

The back room of our cottage, like the front, was an open grid of two-by-four studs, the walls in many places showing the points of nails that held shingles fast to the outside. The studs served all summer as shelves where my seashell and starfish collections accumulated. An ordinary chest of drawers and an equally ordinary armoire with peeling veneer were, except for the beds, the only furniture.

Despite its simplicity, I would not have traded that place for any other in town, not even the custom-designed and -built house high on a sand dune at the westernmost edge of town — a house grand by Provincetown standards — that hosted evening soirees for artists that were talked about for weeks after. No, I would not have traded our little cottage and its perfect location, the freedom it gave me, for any other place in town.

  Provincetown is a town made for boats. Look on a map — P-Town is that triangle of sand tethered to the ragged, jagged arm protruding from the southeastern Massachusetts coast. From neighboring Truro, Provincetown spirals north, northwest, southwest, south, and east, boxing the compass as a mariner would say. It floats in ocean and air, the weight of the world lifted from its shoulders, like the experience one has in a boat.

Without a boat, not only do you miss out on the sheer pleasure of navigating in an exceptionally beautiful, safe, and obstructionless harbor, but you also never gain the perspective, physically and emotionally, that being out on the water affords. The town itself is congested, especially during the summer when the population swells to ten times the year-round population, with everyone vying for space in a place that is but two nautical miles long and a quarter as wide. From Commercial Street, one of two parallel thoroughfares that are laced together, ladderlike, by narrow side streets, you get glimpses — but only glimpses — of the harbor through weathered, tightly set-together houses and former fishermen's sheds, now rental cottages.

But from a boat, it is a different town entirely. In a boat, you are enveloped in light and air. You see the mostly modest wooden A-frame structures strung out like a rambling sentence along a sweep of golden sand that carries on beyond the town proper, dotted at last by a simple white lighthouse at the tip of Long Point. In a boat, you see the subtle undulations of the land, the hills — Gull and Telegraph and Chip in the west end, Town Hill in the center, Gilboa, the great sand dune, in the east. And you are one with that great tidal process, drawn out, nudged in. You notice that many of the homes are oriented to the harbor, built before Commercial Street — or Front Street as it is called by the locals — was laid out in 1835, built during a time when the harbor was Main Street and families watched for their returning fisherman husbands, fathers, and sons to steam around the Point. This is a town shaped by the tides, not only geologically and economically but demographically. Tides of people — immigrants and artists, writers and iconoclasts, itinerants, hippies and homosexuals — have washed ashore over the decades.

Unlike the rest of Cape Cod, Provincetown does not owe its existence to the final Pleistocene ice sheet, known as the Wisconsin Stage Glacier, which began slipping across the landscape 50,000 to 70,000 years ago and retreated some 12,000 years ago. The glacial moraine that resulted from the melting ice ends at High Head in Truro. Provincetown is the product of shore drifting, the movement of sand — supplied by erosion of the long, steep glacial slope that forms the Cape's outer shore — by waves, grain over grain. After High Head, it is all sand, endlessly shifting and extending sand.

The dunes, windswept, desolate, sculpted by nature, are a vast ocean of curving, upward sweeps of sand whose lee slopes reminded writer Elizabeth Reynard of ships' prows. They move forward relentlessly, grain by grain, overtaking anything in their way — cottages, shrubs, entire forests — unless stabilized by beach grass. The grass, without which Provincetown would have long ago washed away, thrives in pure sand. A network of thick stems that run horizontally just below the surface takes root every few inches, sending up slender, rigid blades that catch the sand and grow upward, helping to stabilize the dune vertically. Once stabilized, the sand becomes home to a succession of vegetation, from shrubs to forest. Any topsoil in Provincetown has been imported, and it is always worth acknowledging what Provincetowners have managed to accomplish despite their precarious foothold.

⑥ Our foothold, A Home at Last, was a busy little spot and, next door across the alley, so was Sal's Place. There was history tucked away in our little neighborhood — not the kind of history that fills school textbooks, but local history, history that despite its smallness fits somewhere in the grand plan. Flyer's house, across the street from Sal's, had been the home of Captain Marion Perry, skipper of the *Rose Dorothea,* Provincetown's famous fishing schooner that had won the Lipton Cup in 1907. Flyer, a raconteur and master boatbuilder, spent years building a scale model of the *Rose Dorothea* at the Heritage Museum downtown. Perhaps he had been inspired by the skipper's ghost, returned to finish an undone task. Up on Chip Hill at Cottage and Tremont

Streets, a mid-nineteenth-century excavation had uncovered a stone wall with a shell-lime mortar, an earthen floor, and the remains of a fireplace, proof enough (as far as the locals were concerned) that Norsemen had arrived at the headland long before the Pilgrims had dropped anchor, indeed long before the Englishman Bartholomew Gosnold, visiting in 1602, had found ample enough stocks of codfish to name the place Cape Cod.

The handsome colonial at 76 Commercial Street had been the home of noted marine artist and national academician Frederick Waugh and, after his death, Hans Hofmann, the German expressionist whose Friday critique sessions became something of a happening, attracting notables from the art world as well as tourists. Next door to the Waugh house — if your taste in art leaned toward the traditional, it was the Waugh house; toward the modern, it was the Hofmann house — there was an unusual eight-sided house, designed to better protect against storms and built by a sea captain. I knew it as the Hatchway, a rest home. The West End Racing Club was across the street from that. The Wharf Theater — the second attempt to establish a permanent summer theater — had teetered here, where the racing club sat, on an old, rotting wharf from 1925 until taken by the sea during a 1941 storm.

Number 72, the Seth Nickerson House, a full Cape built about 1750, billed itself as "The Oldest House." The Cape Cod–style building, flawless in proportion, honest in design, was Provincetown's answer to the windswept sands and swirling salt spray. Capes were scattered all over town, tucked in between examples of Italianate and Greek Revival, French Second Empire and Queen Anne, some fronting on the street, others gable-ended. Crouched close to the ground to conserve heat, shingled and muted silver-gray on the sides, clapboarded and blanched on the facade, the Cape's small-paned windows, steeply pitched roof, and massive center chimney were practical features that harmonized to give the style the precision and subtle elegance of Greek architecture.

With its Sandwich glass windows, pegged and hand-hewn beams, wide plank floors, and beehive oven, the Seth Nickerson House could truthfully make claim to being *one* of the oldest houses in town, although some disputed that it was, in fact, *the* oldest. But no other homeowners put the same effort into promoting their "oldest house" as Jack and Adelaide Gregory did their Oldest House (offering tourists a guided tour for a small fee), so to the Seth Nickerson went the appellation.

∽ My world, in the years before the downtown lured me away, could be measured in mere yards. Standing on our deck, if I stretched my arms out, way out, I could just about gather in the space where I spent most of my time. Every so often I wandered a bit afield, and it is precisely because those times were so few that I remember them. If you want to impress something on the memory, I figure that there are two ways to do it: do something so often that it is branded onto the memory, like a leitmotif. Or do something so infrequently that the experience stands out, like an operatic aria.

On my left was the cold storage, the falling-into-ruin fish freezer, appended to the also-falling-into-ruin wharf. On my right was the West End Racing Club. Just under my bedroom window, Commercial Street marked another boundary. And Long Point, the very tip of Cape Cod, about a mile across the harbor, was the outermost edge of my wanderings. Eventually, I outgrew those digs, but for years it was within that rectangle of space that my summer days and nights happily unfolded.

The lingering impression that I have of those days and nights is that they were entirely unstructured and un-supervised, that I came and went at my leisure, that nei-ther parents nor any other adult was anywhere to be found. They were, of course, watching my every move. I just didn't know it. My mother might be up on the deck reading or out on the beach or flats painting, but she had her eye on me. Always.

As for the impression that my days were unstructured, unhurried, they were, as were everyone else's in Province-town, at least during the summer. I never spent a winter in Provincetown, so I can't say how folks organized their time in the off-season, but my hunch, though only a hunch, is that life in general in Provincetown, no matter what the season, is a little less structured, a little more in-formal, than it is elsewhere. Structure, or lack of, is some-thing that goes to one's essential character, like optimism or pessimism, tardiness or promptness. For me, that lack of structure, the spontaneity of every hour, was part of the town's appeal.

No matter what the weather or the tide, there was never a day that the neighborhood kids, town kids as well as all of us summer visitors, did not swim, swim until our fingers and toes wrinkled like prunes, until we had had a gutful of salt water, until the bottoms of our feet were cleaner than if pumiced for weeks, until our teeth chat-tered even though the air temperature was near 90 de-grees. The only thing I remember doing more than swimming was walking. If we were not traveling by boat or bike, we were walking, a leisurely, sauntering, slumping, rolling, rubbery kind of walk that let the air gently lift our hair and circulate through our T-shirts, a walk that really was not intended to get us anywhere, although occasion-ally it did.

Below A Home at Last, the high tide came crawling up the beach, wrapping around the pilings of the restaurant patio just below our deck. Appended to the patio was Sal's wharf, a mere stub of the original Union Wharf that had been built in 1830 or thereabouts (thereabouts is always close enough in Provincetown) for boat repair. In my father's day it was Manny Furtado's boatyard, busy, alive with Portuguese color. During my childhood, though the boatyard was gone, Sal's Place was no less lively and no less colorful, dressed as it was in the colors of Italy. Behind the restaurant, a handful of simple summer apartments, once used for storage and rigging, caulking and painting, lined up on the wharf.

When the tide was high, we might toss coins into the water and dive in after them, hoping to pluck them from their free fall. Better yet, we let the coins fall and then donned mask and snorkel to survey the sea floor, looking for their glint amid shells and glass and seaweed. Or we could dive and cannonball from the wharf into eight or nine feet of water. For the somewhat daring — and I counted myself one of them — the end of the wharf offered a thick plank, with no spring to it but, nevertheless, a diving board of sorts that let us soar through the air in a swan dive or tuck and tumble off in a front or back flip. The truly foolhardy — and I was never one of these — could shinny up a high piling, grab onto the makeshift flagpole steady themselves, and make a leap that sent the heart and pulse racing. Everyone else was content to jump or dive off the boat ramp, whose low end hovered maybe a foot above the water except at the highest tides, when the water lapped up against and over it.

Sal's double-ender dory, painted like the Italian flag, was anchored just offshore. Flyer's little boats tooled around the harbor, shuttling tourists to and from rented rowboats and motorboats. Portuguese mothers toting blankets, picnic baskets, umbrellas, and sun-browned children with dip nets, toy boats, and pails and shovels drifted from side streets, lanes, and grassy footpaths down to the small square of beach between Flyer's and Sal's. A few older folks, always in bathing caps, stood at the water's edge, taking in the scene before taking the plunge.

We'd pass hours playing rag tag, playing to our physical exhaustion. Whenever the tide is up and the sun is beating down, I still think of rag tag and how, as kids, we would tread in water just over our heads, waiting for the knotted, tattered, soaking rag to hurtle itself with a water-splattering *thwack* to the side of someone's head. The object of the game was simply to avoid being hit by the rag by ducking or dodging; if the rag missed its intended target, whoever was "it" had to retrieve the rag and try again.

When they weren't getting tourists acquainted with their rental boat, the kids working for Flyer would swim over to join in. Flyer's son, Arthur Joe, who was my age, could make the swim entirely underwater, disappearing off his ramp and resurfacing, much to our surprise, in the midst of us. He was like some kind of merman, more at home in the water than on terra firma. My mother remembers him barely out of diapers, tooling around the harbor alone in a motorboat, his parents keeping a watchful eye from the beach. His playtime with us was never long (and I often forgot that not everyone was on vacation). His mother would holler a long, drawn-out *Arrrthurrrjoooe,* and he would be off underwater to resume his work. Other kids would trickle in from the neighborhood — the Meads brothers, Larry and Russell from up the street, and Randy and Joady Valentine from across the street. There was magic in that diverse group of kids yoking themselves together, spontaneously and with no adult interference, passing the hours with so very little, letting the game and the day take us where they would.

There were no teams. No loyalty. It was every kid for himself. A few of our players had perfected the fake throw, which sent the targeted rag recipient ducking under water only to surface in the crosshairs. You were dead. There was no way to resubmerge fast enough to avoid the rag. We'd heighten the excitement and the surprise (and give ourselves a rest from treading water) by swimming under the wharf and turning the game into hide-and-seek rag tag, lurking behind pilings or in the deep shadows, buried in the water up to our noses.

While I waited under there to be found, I'd cling to a piling, watching the barnacles just beneath the water's surface, their double doors opening and closing, their feathery feet siphoning food out of the water. Above the water's surface, the barnacles were closed tight, waiting for the tide to come in still higher so that they, too, could be nourished. Their limestone shells were volcanic in shape with ferociously sharp edges. The small lacerations that they inflicted on me bled profusely and, it seemed, forever, dispersing wisps of my blood into the water.

Sharing the pilings with the barnacles were tiny, dun-colored periwinkles grazing on algae, along with clumps of rockweed. Seawater filled the yellowy bladders of the rockweed, commonly called bladderweed, buoying it and fanning it gracefully in the water. Many of the pilings were grooved, honeycombed by shipworms, streaked with smooth green algae, stained by the rust from bolts, blackened to where the tide rose twice daily. The oldest pilings were actual tree trunks, many still encased in bark, the knobs where branches had been attached still visible. As the original pilings deteriorated, they were replaced by telephone poles — smooth, dark brown, coated with creosote to protect against the destructive shipworm, a mollusk that survives by eating wood. Those pilings lacked all of the character of their forebears.

The sunlight stole in under the wharf, glinting off the water's surface, turning it a dancing yellowy-green. The air was cool and clammy, the sounds amplified. I'd move silently from piling to piling, bursting bladderweed between my fingers, bubbling the water with my mouth, picking periwinkles and watching their little doors slam shut, looking out at the bright sunlight, listening to the voices that seemed to have forgotten I was part of the game.

Then, *thwack!* The rag found me smack on the side of the head.

The game went on as long as the tide allowed, but as certainly as the tide had come crawling up the beach, it was drawn back out, out from around the pilings, out from under Flyer's orange-and-white dories with their little black outboards, out, out, like a huge tarpaulin being pulled back, exposing the harbor floor, small plots of which we had become intimate with at the high tide by way of mask and snorkel.

Some days, my friends and I would follow the tide out, searching for enough water to do our handstands or float on our backs. We might commandeer a boat, anchored far enough offshore that there was still enough water to dive or jump in. More often, though, when it came, I relished the low tide, the harbor without its watery cover, a world made small, a Lilliput where I was Gulliver.

The flats looked like sugar cookies spread out on a baking sheet. With the sea drained, each ashen grain of sand held the heat of the summer sun, and I often would lie on my back in the middle of a flat, staring deep into the blue sky, convinced that there was life out there. Why should we be the only ones? My favorite television show was *Lost in Space*, and more than anything, I wanted to be Angela Cartwright, Penny Robinson, wanted to be part of her delicious adventure, wanted to be on the *Jupiter II* hurtling toward Alpha Centauri, thrown off course by Dr. Smith's sabotage and shipwrecked on an uncharted planet. Their year was 1997 (how far in the future that seemed) and their world was a "futuristic" one of rocket belts, jet packs, lasers, hydroponic gardens, cryogenics, and robots.

✍ I had purchased a small telescope with paper-route money and took it every summer to Provincetown, where I trained it on terrestrial as well as celestial objects. The flat, broad expanse of the harbor made for ideal viewing of the distant Truro and Wellfleet shores, for dropping in on an inbound fishing boat or beachcombers out at Long Point. In the heavens I saw stars that looked red or blue and planets that looked like tiny oyster crackers, floating in a great bowl of black soup. But mostly I looked at the moon — not the luminous and corpulent dinner plate moon whose tenant with the furrowed brow looked down sad-eyed, but the crescent moon on whose shadow lines I could see craters, mountains, and waterless seas.

My guts tingled when I peeked at the moon, but my first glimpse of Saturn left me breathless, my heart pounding. Never mind that countless other people had seen it and seen it better and bigger. I had just discovered it.

I thrilled at being able to navigate the celestial sphere as I did my neighborhood, to recognize a point of light as I would a neighbor. I didn't need to understand what I was looking at, the science of it all. It was enough just to look, with the naked eye, with binoculars, with my simple telescope, each tool enabling me to overcome a little more of the darkness. Rachel Carson well understood that sense of wonder when she wrote, "If facts are the seeds that later produce knowledge and wisdom, then the emotions and the impressions of the senses are the fertile soil in which the seeds must grow." I knew how many, many more points of light were out there beyond my reach, windows that I could not yet see through, but perhaps someday would. Whether probing the deep blue of afternoon or the endless black of night, there was then, in childhood, something exhilarating and life-affirming in letting myself be lured out there.

⑥ There were never many clouds in the Provincetown sky. At least that is the way I remember it, not like at home where we could lie in the grass and go on safari, watching puffs, wisps, and fish scales gather into giraffes, elephants, and lions who galloped off across the Serengeti. No, in Provincetown, there was just an aggregate of blues against which terns and gulls flashed their whites and hovered and glided. Except for their jabbering, maybe a halyard tapping out a message on a wooden sailboat mast, the harbor was quiet. Boats were keeled over on the sand, their ropes and buoys deployed haphazardly by the outgoing tide.

Yet it was hardly lifeless out on this great sea floor. Tidal runs scoured canyons in and serpentined around the flats, their cool current carrying periwinkles and dogwinkles, drills and darting sand shrimp — what we called tickle fish — and scavenging crabs. A discarded wine bottle grew flowing green seaweed tresses. We might find a scallop, alive, its rows of tiny blue eyes just inside its shells encircling the mantle that secretes the shell. We would pry it open just enough to peek in and glimpse the small white, much-esteemed, edible adductor muscle lodged amid the heart and rectum and gills. Or maybe we'd find a pearl. We hoped. When we would return the scallop to the water, it would clap its shells together and jet off.

Hermit crabs, scavengers and squatters, scurried about in their fuzz-encrusted houses. The fuzz, called snail fur, is a colony of hydroids, tiny animals found only on shells occupied by hermit crabs, a kind of squatter on the squatter. If we were lucky, we would catch a hermit crab in the act of making his quick move to a roomier residence. After fastidiously looking over the available real estate and settling on something he could grow into, the hermit crab would withdraw from his old abode — making himself momentarily vulnerable — and back his withered-looking lower body, without hesitation, into the spiral of the new shell. A perfect fit. For the moment.

Gulls scurried across the flats, leaving behind feathers of down and a frenzy of triangular footprints embossed in the sand. Strands of eelgrass and bits of seaweed — reds and greens and browns, branched and tufted, lacey, leafy, and elongated, coarse and silky — fringed the flats. The tide had left behind proof of its most recent visit: swash marks, ripples, rills. Sea worms revealed their subterranean existence by ribbonlike tracks flowing from their front doors, by coiled heaps of sand on the flats, and by short, tubed membranes, camouflaged with shells and seaweed, projecting above the flats. There were shells of all sorts: hat-shaped limpets, quahogs, razors, blue mussels, fluted bay scallops, glossy jingle shells, ragged oysters, piggy-backing boat shells, whorled whelks — and, for me, the prize of them all, tumbled in by offshore storms, the deep-sea scallop, smooth, fan-shaped, carrying a pink-tinged radiating sunrise on its shell.

It was inevitable that I would begin collecting, tucking shells into my bathing suit or finding a large sea clamshell that could serve as my collection dish. My sights would be trained on the sea floor, searching and searching so I wouldn't miss a single object. I could become hopelessly lost in this beachcombing, oblivious to anything going on around me, unaware of the direction my wanderings were taking me, pulling me farther and farther away from the restaurant, our cottage, Flyer's. The women and children on the beach with their picnics and colorful beach umbrellas would become mere specks to me.

I could always rely on a soft-shelled clam, what many know as a steamer or a longneck — and what the locals call, more colorfully, a piss clam — to spit up a geyser from inside the flat. Siphoning food and disposing waste, his tiny hole gave him away. I dropped my treasures and dug with both hands, carefully raking up the creature so as not to break his brittle shell, then buried him again. Camouflaged in the ashen flats was a sand dollar, sun-bleached and delicately etched with a five-petaled flower. I coveted the sand dollars, as I did the deep-sea scallop, infrequent arrivals to the inner harbor.

My wandering would take me to the water's edge, where the ebbing tide had come to rest and would remain, momentarily, before turning around and beginning its long crawl back in across the flats. I'd wade out, surprised by pockets of cooler water, waist-deep in search of moon snails, a common spiral-shell mollusk that left erratic trails in the sand. I'd pluck the snail from the water and watch it pull its enormous fleshy foot back into the shell, never believing that it would all fit as snugly as it did.

Deposited on the sea floor were sand collars, the moon snail's egg cases. If I held the collar up to the light, I could see the eggs embedded between grains of sand. As elegant as these collars were, I soon learned that they could not survive long out of the water. The collars dried and disintegrated. And so I returned them to the sea.

With the rising tide, I retreated to the flats where any number of creatures had been stranded by the tide. I often came upon sea robins, their fins spread open like fans, or skates, a nuisance to all but a few of the local fishermen who had discovered that the wings made pretty good eating, and horseshoe crabs, those awkward, ancient creatures — more closely related to spiders than to crabs — that have changed little in 300 million years. I was always fascinated by these creatures, lifting them by the tail and watching their legs flailing, their breathing gills undulating. For several summers I found coins, usually quarters, lodged between the gills, scooped up, I figured, as they plowed the sands. To this day, I amuse myself by checking the flaps of horseshoe crabs in much the same way that others might flip down the coin return of a public phone.

Scattered, too, on the flats were dogfish, members of the shark family, their sleek, gray carcasses stinking in the summer sun. And squid, another odd-looking creature, not a fish but a shellfish, with the ability to camouflage its rubbery and projectile-shaped body. It was hard to believe that folks in town actually enjoyed cooking and eating them, slicing the flaccid body into chewy ringlets. We squeezed them, fascinated by their texture and inky emission, and chopped off the arms and tentacles for fishing bait.

I never knew how much time had passed out there on the flats. My only clock all those summers in Provincetown was the noon fire whistle. The blinding white sun that stood me in a puddle of my shadow when I set out would soften and bronze, dropping toward the horizon, throwing my shadow, long and lithe, sideways across the flats. Laden with sea-borne treasures, my bathing suit dried by the day's warmth, my body whitened by sea salt, I'd make my way back to shore, lost still in my beachcoming.

The tide would catch up to me, and my legs would push against the rising water. A school of feed fish, thick in the shallows, headed toward me, zigging, zagging, and continuing on its way. It was the abundance of fish, fish of all sorts, that had made Provincetown a prosperous little village so many decades earlier.

⚓ The town was a Yankee enclave — names like Nickerson, Soper, Rich, and Miller filling out the local directory — until the early nineteenth century, when the Portuguese, who would imprint Provincetown with a lasting character and color, arrived as crews on Yankee-owned whaling vessels. Later, Grand Banks and Georges Bank cod fishing brought another influx of Portuguese from the mainland and the Azores. By the end of the century the fishing fleet numbered nearly 300 vessels.

During my childhood, the Portuguese family-owned fleet was still healthy, a collection of draggers that worked the nutrient-rich waters of Georges Banks, 100 miles out to sea. The harvest of flounder, haddock, whiting, and cod was still plentiful and could provide a decent living for captain and crew, although it could not begin to compare to the boom years of a century earlier when fishing schooners, whalers, and the 100-vessel mackerel fleet choked the harbor and made Provincetown the preeminent Grand Banks port.

Back then, the beach was studded with salt-works windmills that pumped seawater through hollowed-out logs and into vats where it was evaporated by the sun. Used to preserve fish, marine salt proved a profitable business for Provincetown until salt deposits were discovered in New York.

On the wharves and beaches, in front yards and back yards, every available space was given over to slatted drying tables called flake racks on which the laborious business of curing cod, what the locals called "making fish," was carried out. Cleaned and soaked in brine, the fish were spread open on the racks in the morning, allowed to dry all day under the sun, and then covered or taken in at night (to escape the moisture-heavy night air and soaking morning dew), only to be uncovered or returned to the racks the next morning. After two or three days, the fish was "made." It would then keep for months and could be shipped long distances.

The completion of the Old Colony Railroad in 1873, and the perfected design of the large fishing schooners brought the fresh fishery, and the demise of the salt fishery, to Provincetown. Arriving iced-down from the Grand Banks, packed in ice blocks cut from Provincetown's ponds, fish could be shipped by rail that same day to Boston, Baltimore, Philadelphia, and New York. The sleek schooners that Provincetown was famous for, such as the *Rose Dorothea*, made a contest of delivering their catches, racing one another to Boston and then back to Provincetown for fresh bait before returning to the Grand Banks. Bait fish from the traps that was not used fresh on the schooners was taken to the cold storages and frozen into blocks.

⑥ At one time in Provincetown there had been more than fifty wharves, a few as long as 1,200 feet, some with marine railways long enough to haul out the grandest of the Grand Banks vessels. They were work spaces, extensions of the narrow beach, crowded with the drying racks and the lofts and sheds of sail makers, net menders, painters, caulkers, and blacksmiths. During my childhood, most of that activity was passing into history, and the lofts and sheds were undergoing the transformation to summer apartments and artists' studios.

I remember a handful of working wharves, most in dis-
repair but not yet ready to relinquish their usefulness.
They would have been eyesores anywhere else, but in
Provincetown they were keepsakes from a disappearing
time — long, narrow groves of spindly pilings topped with
planking, lurching out into the harbor. Freeman's Wharf, a
few doors down from Sal's on the crook in Commercial
Street, was one of the working wharves, appended to the
cold storage and reaching out into the harbor to meet the
draggers returning from the fishing grounds. By the time
the boats rounded Long Point, the catch for the most part
had been sorted and culled of trash fish, spider crabs,
starfish, and seaweed, and much of the heading and gut-
ting had been done. I was alerted to an incoming boat by a
frenzied entourage of seagulls that escorted every catch,
gorging on the offal that was tossed overboard.

Whatever I was doing, I would stop. I'd fix my eyes on
the end of the wharf and watch the catch from the draggers being loaded into a box towed by a gasoline-powered
tram car that labored along a narrow-gauge track. The fish
train would make its way in toward the trap shed at the
head of the wharf, where the catch was manually unloaded
and reloaded into buckets. With seawater draining and the
occasional fish sliding off the pile and falling to the beach
(where a few town kids had gathered in anticipation of
just such an event), the bucket was hoisted up a clacking
aerial cableway to a wide opening on the top level, where a
fish packer in a rubber apron reached out and hauled it in.

按 For decades earlier, it had been trap boats unloading
their catch of bait fish at the end of the wharf. As other
generations watched whaling and long-lining come to an
end, my generation watched as inshore trap fishing, which
once boasted more than fifteen boats and more than 100

weirs all along the inshore waters from Wellfleet to Provincetown, closed out an era. After being a way of life for more than a century, its last vestiges were a few traps out in the harbor, in the cove and off Long Point, the trap shed next to Freeman's, and the huge cold-storage facility, the last of Provincetown's five freezers. The trap boat *Carlotta* was still afloat, but her sister, *Charlotte,* had been abandoned on the beach next to the Provincetown Inn, where she was slowly being swallowed by the sand.

Trap fishing, or weir fishing as it is sometimes called, was practiced by Native Americans and began commercially during the mid-1800s to meet the constant demand for fresh bait fish — herring and mackerel — on the cod schooners, which set out miles of line with baited hooks at measured intervals. By World War I, diesel-powered draggers towing baglike trawls were displacing long-liners. With little need then for bait fish, trap fishermen directed their efforts to food fish — tuna and whiting — to keep the industry, and the cold storages, viable. Bought cheap and frozen during the summer, fish could be sold off-season at a considerable profit when demand was high.

Atlantic Coast Fisheries owned most of the cold storages, trap boats, and traps that were set out on leased areas as granted by the state. Trap fishermen, employed by Atlantic Coast Fisheries, split their catch fifty-fifty. As fishing goes, trap fishing, although monotonous and back-breaking work, had advantages over its deep-sea relative. Trap fishermen began at dawn, drawing the traps once a day, sometimes two or three times if they were producing. Sometimes the fish were so plentiful that they were given away or released to keep prices up. Most days, after delivering their catch, the fishermen were home by early afternoon. The traps took about a week to set in the spring, another week to dismantle in December. Trap fishermen spent the winter months onshore, mending and tarring nets and repairing the trap boat, while the draggermen toiled at sea.

Ask ten folks why trap fishing declined and you'll get ten answers: the migratory patterns and cycles of fish; the depletion of stocks; pollution; changing water temperature; draggers working inshore, churning up the sea bed, disturbing the spawning grounds; competition from foreign fishing vessels; pleasure boats tangling in the weirs; escalating insurance and equipment costs; falling fish prices; even the Cape Cod Canal currents. And probably all should shoulder some blame. The real villain, though, was time. The harvesting of fish was changing. The only place for trap fishing in the modern world was in memories and family scrapbooks. Dragging for fish in colorful, family-owned boats would meet the same fate a generation later when factory ships and quotas would change the face of fishing forever.

⑥ When I'd putter in my motorboat past the last remnants of the weirs out in the harbor, the fixed-pole traps looked like haphazard, even abandoned, arrangements of dozens of spindly poles draped with mesh and line that resembled cobwebs. In fact, the hickory poles were carefully configured, an assembly designed to lure schooling fish to captivity. It all seemed arcane to me, until Joe Corea explained everything.

Joe Corea was something of a neighborhood legend. Everyone knew him. He was Joe Cow to his friends, and most everyone was his friend. How he got his nickname, I don't know, but most townies had one, earned for some deed, notorious or otherwise, and handed down from father to son. Joe had been a commercial fisherman, but by the time we came to town, he was working up-Cape for the state and fishing for pleasure. He lived across the street from Sal's, one door up on Cottage Street, with his wife, Florence, who made the best blueberry pie and carrot cake I have ever tasted. Every evening Joe sat on his fence at the Commercial Street end of his sandy vacant strip where Sal's dinner patrons could park. Back then, in the seventies, I think it was a dollar to park, maybe even fifty cents. Joe was supposed to collect the money, but more often than not, he was absorbed in animated conversation with one of us, Flyer, or some passerby, unaware that a car had slipped into a spot behind him and that the hungry dinner guests were making off without paying. When that happened, Florence, who saw everything from the house, would come charging down Cottage Street and deliver a feisty reprimand to Joe. She had no qualms about chasing down the perpetrators and getting her due. Florence and Joe were then probably in their late fifties. Their sons were grown.

Joe took my younger brother, Johnny, under his wing and taught him all that anyone needed to know about fishing. "If you want to know how, ask Joe Cow," Joe would say, or "I've rung more salt water out of my gloves than most people have sailed over," he'd boast. We loved that kind of talk.

In the early morning mist and the first pink of day, Johnny would rendezvous with Joe at Sal's ramp. They'd mosey off in Joe's outboard, *Two Pals*, across a silent harbor to Pamet in Truro for a thermos of coffee and a box of Danish, then steam across the bay for striped bass before the fish deserted the surface. Bass are creatures of habit, lying on bars, biting certain things and ignoring everything else while their taste buds are so primed, and avoiding strong sunlight. Joe and Johnny would be gone all day, fishing inshore spots that had proved lucrative on previous trips, crossing paths with other local fanatics.

There was no shortage of fish talk — a kind of vague shorthand that every fisherman understood — exchanged between the boats.

"Whaddaya hear?"

"Good striper action with plugs off Lecount's and the Race."

"Nothing at Ryder's. Goddam blues are chasing everything."

"Any fluke?"

"Hatches is producing on sand eels."

"I hear Dickie hooked up. Second one this week."

Like poker players, they bluffed and were circumspect, never letting anyone come alongside, never letting anyone see their catch. An unspoken competition among these fishermen and a decent price for bass turned their sport into serious business. Precisely where the stripers were biting, if these fishermen were lucky enough to have found the spot, and precisely what they were biting remained secrets.

Depending on where Joe and Johnny cast their lines, I could sometimes locate them with binoculars or my telescope. I followed their trolling around the bay or out in the cove, followed their homeward journey, around Long Point, their exhausted faces and low-riding boat a sure sign that the bass had been running and that it had been a good day. Stripers were plentiful in those years, and it was not unusual for Joe and Johnny to bring home dozens of fish — thirty- and forty-pounders, handsome with their blue-greens, their dark stripes and clear gold eyes, covering the deck of the boat. I used to tease Joe that the fish had probably been grabbed off the beach after falling from the cold-storage buckets. Sal usually bought the catch and put the steaks and fillets on the menu the next night. Not many years later, the bass vanished for well over a decade, prompting strict regulations about quotas and size. Although some say the fish are back better than ever, the days of filling a boat are gone for good. The daily allowance has dropped to one fish.

Joe took me fishing only once — at twilight, across to Ryder Beach off Truro. All we caught that night, as Joe used to like to say, was cold, but it is an evening that I remember vividly because it was the only time I have ever looked upon Provincetown after dark from out on the bay, beyond Long Point. On the boat ride home, I searched for that most familiar of landmarks, the steady green beacon at Long Point superimposed on the empty, dark, distant shore, which was how it showed itself to me night after night when I viewed it from my terrestrial perch at A Home at Last. I had never considered how it would look when viewed from the other side. From out on the bay, it was no longer a landmark; instead, it was just one lamp of thousands, indistinguishable from the other festive greens that decorated the Provincetown shoreline.

During this, my only real fishing trip with Joe, he showed me a thing or two about casting, showed me how to gut and fillet a fish, taught me a bunch of cuss words in Portuguese, and showed me just what went on inside the traps.

We followed the leader, a 700- to 800-foot curtain of mesh that ran offshore at a right angle to the shore. When confronted by such an obstacle, schooling fish use a sixth sense called a lateral line — a row of hair-lined pores — to sense and avoid the obstruction. The lateral line also keeps the fish school orderly and together. At the leader, the school turns instinctively and swims parallel to the leader to deeper water, following the leader to the heart of the trap and ultimately into its bowl, a wide oval tarred net held on the sea bed by weights. The bowl acts as a holding pen where the fish swim freely in figure eights until the trap men close and gather the net in, working the fish into a smaller and smaller area. The smaller fish are bailed with nets called kill devils, and the larger are gaffed into the hold of the five-man trap boat, a particularly handsome vessel made especially for this work, with flowing lines and a capacious hold.

When we were parallel to the leader, the design of the trap became evident. The creosote-painted poles, hydraulically staked in ten feet of sea bed and in up to forty feet of water, rose twenty to thirty feet above us. The draped netting was strewn with bits of seaweed, crisscrossed overhead by lines hung with blocks. We didn't go into the trap — a no-no of arrestable proportion — but instead trolled around the outside, where an eerie stillness settled over us. Inside, below the surface quiet, an underwater struggle was taking place, bass or dogfish, butterfish or blue, squid, whiting, tuna (which is sometimes called horse mackerel, and which could tear the nets to shreds), strays and oddities frantically searching for a way out. The trap was designed so that fish trying to leave were directed back in. They were doomed unless deemed useless (trash fish) and tossed back by the fishermen. Many were labeled trash fish in those days, including the dogfish now overfished to satisfy England's fish-and-chips appetite. In the stillness of the next morning's sunrise, when the fishermen entered and pursed the net, the fish would learn their fate.

◈ In his youth, my father had worked at the cold storage, and when I was young, he was still friendly with some of the fish packers. He'd take me there occasionally to watch the assembly-line operation, which began with the dumping of an avalanche of fish, mostly whiting, into a large hopper. From there, they would move onto a convey-or belt, where the last of the entrails was removed. The place would reek. There'd be water everywhere, water to wet down the fish, water to keep the fish moving on their way, water to wash down the floors that were strewn with roe, scales, and blood. Laid in metal pans, head to tail, the fish would be sent downstairs, compacted, flash-frozen into blocks, and packed and shipped out in refrigerated trucks, or stored, waiting for higher market prices.

We would never leave empty-handed. My father would be given a little something to take home for the frying pan. I never ate fish — never acquired a taste for it — but there was something appealing about those visits to the cold storage, something exciting about casting my line out under Joe's watchful eye, something pleasurable about running my hand along the cool, smooth, graceful, tapered shape of the fish, something exhilarating about catching my own fish.

Every child should know that feeling of dropping a line weighted down by a small bit of lead, watching it drop below the surface, and then waiting and wondering what might grab it. A few times every summer my father would take my brothers and me out onto the cold-storage wharf, where we'd each drop a hand line weighted down with a sil-ver mackerel jig. Sometimes we used a gizmo called an um-brella rig, a device with four arms that let us fish with four jigs. Our little fishing rig was as simple as could be — no rod, no reel, no casting skills required, just a plastic yellow handle, string, and a hook. We would lie on our bellies, staring down over the edge of the wharf into our own re-flections, down to where our jigs glinted. The dense school would come, cutting a dark swath through the water. The fish would bite, the line tremble. I'd jig, the weight on the end of the line evidence of my conquest. As I wrapped the line carefully around the plastic handle, there would still be fight on the other end, sometimes enough for the fish to spit the hook and make an escape, especially if I let the line go slack for an instant. The fish would be ready to take advantage of my lapse. Those who had no chance for escape would still fight the brave fight, darting sideways in flowing Zs, yanking at the line, bursting through the surface, snapping their greenish and blue and silvery bodies, gasping with their red gills long after being pulled from the water.

The process of recollection that we undertake as adults is a lot like fishing. We drop our line, not really knowing what we might hook onto. Some memories are pulled in easily, with little fight, others not so willingly, churning just below the surface, reluctant to show themselves. We get a glimpse of some memories only to lose them in a moment. Some, we prefer to lose. And then there are all those memories, schooling about in the depths, that we will not hook this time, maybe never.

Sal's Place

SAL'S PLACE is in the west end of town, Ciro & Sal's, in the east end. The namesake of both places is Salvatore Del Deo, a man of boundless charm and generosity, a man who lives life, as the Italians say, *con amore*. As I write this memoir, he is well into his seventies, still in good health, and still living in Provincetown, although he spends more and more of each winter in his beloved Italy. He is no longer the proprietor of Sal's Place, having sold the restaurant some years ago. But it will always be his place for me and for so many others who were welcomed to the sanctuary he created on his small bit of beachfront, a sanctuary that let childhood survive a little longer than it might have elsewhere.

Sal's friendship with Ciro Cozzi dates back to the late 1940s, when both were art students. In the early 1950s they opened a bistro together, a simple place with cable-spool tables and nail-keg seats that became popular with the artists. By 1960, Sal had struck out on his own, purchasing property in the west end that included A Home at Last as well as a handful of summer apartments. He opened Sal's Place on the stump of the old Union Wharf.

I owe more than happy memories to Sal. In a sense, I owe him my existence because it was he who introduced my parents to each other in New York, where they were married and where I was born. As seventeen-year-olds, Sal and my mother had met at the Vesper George School of Art in Boston. My mother remembers a young man of swarthy, Mediterranean good looks, a perfect pearly smile, and a head full of silky, dark curls. One of her vivid memories is of standing behind Sal in a painting class, she at her easel, he at his, and hearing him humming arias from Verdi operas. He had grown up in Providence, Rhode Island, where his parents had emigrated from the island of Ischia in the Bay of Naples. The family had been desperately poor, but there was a glow about Sal that came from a happy home, the love of a mother and father. He embraced his Italian heritage at a time when others of ethnic backgrounds were denying theirs.

Sal, my mother, and several other Vesper George students learned of Provincetown through Henry Hensche, who, as the disciple of impressionist painter and teacher Charles Hawthorne, had taken over Hawthorne's Cape School of Art upon Hawthorne's death in 1930.

Ⓑ Three decades earlier, in 1899, Hawthorne — painter, son of a sea captain, and former assistant to William Merritt Chase — had put the remote Provincetown on the art map. Painters flocked there, the town's natural assets, its lack of pretension, and *dolce far niente* Mediterranean atmosphere no doubt appealing to their romantic and Spartan natures. Hawthorne implored his students to see the way things came together. Your ability to see is your tool of trade; nothing else matters, he would tell them. For portraits he posed a model in sunlight, the face shaded by an umbrella or hat so that the students could not distinguish the model's features. A mudhead, it was called. He taught color, not drawing, and required that his students work with a palette knife, a clumsy tool that refused to articulate details. Hawthorne's approach to painting was fundamental: concentrate on the big spots of color, get the big shapes and color relationships down correctly, and the drawing would take care of itself. He believed that the first color note was the most important, influencing every other. "Always look for the unexpected in nature," he told his students. "Every day has its own individuality of color. Be humble enough to see as if it were the first time." And every Friday morning when Hawthorne, dressed meticulously all in white, painted for his class, he did just that.

A tide of poets, playwrights, and other writers — Eugene O'Neill, George Cram Cook and Susan Glaspell, John Reed, Mary Heaton Vorse, Hutchins Hapgood and Neith Boyce, Harry Kemp — followed Hawthorne, gathering in one another's homes during the summer of 1915 to read plays aloud. Disillusioned with the commercialism of the American theater of their day, they established their own "little theater" in the east end in an ancient fish house owned by Mary Heaton Vorse at the end of Lewis Wharf. Calling themselves the Provincetown Players, the group pledged to write and produce American plays of "real artistic, literary, and dramatic merit," plays that explored Freud, Marx, sex, and suffrage. During the summer of 1916, they produced O'Neill's first play, *Bound East for Cardiff.*

A second wave of painters and theater people washed ashore after World War I, and by the 1930s, Provincetown's creative roster included Hans Hofmann, Frederick Waugh, Richard Miller, Karl Knaths, Ed Dickinson, Ross Moffett, Gerrit Beneker, George Elmer Browne, and my grandfather, John Whorf.

❧ Living was cheap in those days. Fishermen, generous with their daily catch, and merchants, doctors, dentists, and landlords who accepted payment in works of art staved off artists' privation and kept roofs over their heads. It was during those years, the Depression years, that my grandparents defaulted on their Brookline, Massachusetts, mortgage and fled to Provincetown.

Though my grandfather had grown up in Winthrop on Boston's North Shore, much of his childhood had been spent in Provincetown exploring the dunes and the woods, watching long-liners and trap boats coming and going from the harbor, fishermen unloading their catch and repairing their gear. Little had changed when he returned permanently to Provincetown in the 1930s. A prolific painter, my grandfather learned from Hawthorne the impressionistic brushwork and color that he applied to watercolor, his medium of choice, a spontaneous medium that suited my grandfather's restless temperament. Always, there is light playing over his subjects, humble subjects generally: yellow-slickered fishermen on a drizzly morning, backyard gardens buried in fog, a sailing party under a full summer moon, trap boats riding deep in the water, chickadees in winter-bare branches, the silver-blue-gray winter waterfront, lumber schooners, the village in spring, snow on the dunes. Always straightforward, always the extrovert, my grandfather painted social essays, the world before his eyes. He loved atmosphere. He noticed details — swirls of smoke from chimneys, a hand-painted sign in a window that announced "eggs for sale," a rocker on a porch, a watery sidewalk reflection, whitecaps in the harbor. If there is a secret, aside from his technical virtuosity, to the popular appeal he enjoyed in his too-short life, it is that he reminded people of everyday scenes, of the dignity and tenor of their everyday lives. His subjects are the little, unpretentious things that I, too, remember about Provincetown.

⑥ Henry Hensche's visit to the Vesper George School of Art, where he gave a painting demonstration, enticed many in his audience, including Sal, to make the four-hour journey that summer of 1946 on the narrow road that meandered through a vast dune wilderness. The glowing endorsement they brought back to Boston in the fall encouraged others at the school to follow the next summer, my mother among them. For her, having grown up in a city neighborhood of tenements, packed-dirt backyards, and board fences, Provincetown was paradise despite its own share of poverty and rough edges.

As a student in Provincetown, Sal was introduced to the painter Edwin Dickinson, whom he studied with during the winter months in New York at the Art Students' League. There in Dickinson's class my father met Sal, whom he remembers working fastidiously at his easel, his turpentine in one quahog shell, his linseed oil in another. The shells sparked a conversation, a conversation that eventually worked its way in roundabout fashion to Provincetown, my father's hometown.

Introduced by Sal in New York, where my mother was also a student at the League, my parents were married in New York in 1955 and took an apartment at St. Mark's Place in Greenwich Village. I was born the following June. Fleeing the oppressive heat of New York City, my parents rented a tiny apartment that summer from Ciro Cozzi in Provincetown's east end. There would be a visit to Provincetown every summer thereafter, to various rental cottages, until the late 1970s, an opportunity to see family and friends and, most important for my mother, to stay connected with the art community that she had invested herself in since high school.

I have little recollection of the earliest years, but old black-and-white snapshots, the ones with the deckled edges, show me splashing about at the water's edge, scooting about on the decks of keeled-over sailboats, crawling on shipworm-eaten timbers, wearing Indian headdresses made from seagull feathers. Those few photographs are important to me because they have saved things I have lost — a landscape, a person, a moment, a memory. But I remember the way the days and nights unfolded at Sal's Place.

The restaurant would stir early in preparation for an evening that would see more than 300 dinners served. The bread truck would arrive from up-Cape with cardboard boxes stuffed with fragrant, yeasty, and warm loaves. The produce truck, stacked with crates of ripe melons and peaches, cucumbers and onions, lemons, kiwis, and strawberries, would block traffic out front while being unloaded. Pots, pans, and dishes left over from the night before were loaded noisily into the dishwasher. Victor DeCarlo would arrive to supervise the daytime operation and with him, his redheaded son Tommy, about fourteen at the time, who did prep work in the kitchen. Jimmy Ferreira, a townie who left Provincetown to take a professorship in Michigan but who returned summer after summer, arrived next to make Ischian-style meatballs, with raisins.

Sal was always working, right alongside the hired help, behind the butcher-block counter, in front of the gas burners, every one of them with a high blue flame jumping through the grills. But his real contribution came in making Sal's Place an oasis, a place where young people found direction. Or if not direction, the time and patience they needed to find direction.

The fans would begin to whirl, chasing out the first robust aromas of the day. Sal's wife, Josephine, would arrive and take her place in the front room, tucked in a corner where she managed all the bookkeeping and business affairs. Efficient, watchful, and of a more sober nature, she complemented Sal, who, by his gregarious and romantic nature, might well have given away the store. Jo had just the right balance of kindness and authority to make Sal's Place always feel like family, but a family whose every member knew what was expected. She was always Mrs. Del Deo to me. Sal was always Sal.

Sal and Jo's daughter, Giovanna, was a year younger than I was. A beauty straight out of a Renaissance painting, Gigi was everything I wasn't as a young teenager — sophisticated, graceful, demure, lithe, with flowing brown hair, ringlets framing her face. Every morning she would take her place in the kitchen and create her desserts, works of art really, making a colorful ricotta filling for cannolis, pouring *cassatas* and *zuppa ingleses* into baking dishes. Her brother, Romolo, a cherubic boy, was two years younger than Gigi. Inquisitive and with a keen intellect, with an interest in insects and fish, he would work all day chopping and dicing mushrooms and preparing other ingredients indispensable to the cooks. Both of the kids had a European aura about them, seemed much older than their years. They were always working and often brought their work out onto the patio where I hovered near them, watching, flattered to be invited to help. For me it was great fun, never work, and it made me feel even more a part of the place. From the reel-to-reel, Judy Collins would sing out in a voice as luminous as the Cape Cod light. Or it might be *Porgy and Bess* or something from Verdi or Puccini that inspired someone in the kitchen to test his own tenor voice. Even then, when I was only eleven or twelve, I was aware that while Romolo chopped and Giovanna carefully sliced, my brothers and I, the neighborhood kids, and the kids staying in Sal's apartments were all enjoying ourselves at the end of the wharf, their wharf; but they had little time to play.

Over the years, throughout every morning and into every afternoon, a kaleidoscope of characters would fill the patio, which was built of old ships' timbers combed from the outer beach and hung with baskets of flowers. Some were Sal's old friends in town for a few days. Most were summer folks, regulars like my parents who came to share in the bonhomie that Sal encouraged. A few were Socratic types, contemplating the meaning of life and not at all concerned, it seemed, with answers or certainties. Mrs. Rizk, the mother of artist Ray Rizk whose studio was across the street, and Mrs. Tod, Josephine's mother, would sit shaded under a red, white, and blue Cinzano umbrella, preparing something special for the dinner menu, stuffed zucchini or perhaps stuffed grape leaves. Sal's brother, Frank, might be teaching an Italian lesson. Arthur Cohen might arrive on his bike with his paint box or his home-movie camera. Others would bring the *New Yorker* or *New York Times,* whose front page was choked with reports of riots and rallies, marches and mobs. They'd chat and argue among themselves about events in Southeast Asia. Words that were dissonant to my ear and that meant nothing to me were fired across the tables — Pleiku, Danang, Mekong, Mylai, Haiphong. Capote and Mailer and Updike were the preferred summer reading.

A gangly, middle-aged stranger who worked the carnival circuit, a man we called Larry Hummazoo, strolled onto Sal's patio one morning, carrying a bagful of carny trinkets. We flocked to him, fascinated by the variety of whistles and trills that he produced from his mouth with no apparent instrument or effort. He revealed his secret — a tiny cardboard and cellophane semicircle that he held on the roof of his mouth. Once moistened and softened, it worked in the same way as blowing on a blade of grass between the thumbs. Despite our practice, few of us got beyond the most rudimentary of sounds, managing a little squeak here, another squeak there — certainly no trills and certainly nothing that would fool any of the feathered locals. We had better luck with the hummazoo, a cookie-sized plastic instrument that required only an ability to hum, which we all had. Larry returned for several summers, always with a bag of goodies for us. No one seemed to know much about him, not even his real last name. It just didn't seem to matter.

Francis and Sunday, a married couple who lived downstairs at A Home at Last and who, more than anyone else, reminded us that it was the Age of Aquarius, that God was dead, and that strawberry fields were forever, would sit on the patio fashioning colorful necklaces and bracelets from olive oil can designs. Old-timer Johnny Oliver, a house painter, captivated us with his impassioned retelling of the December 1927 sinking of a Navy S-4 submarine off Wood End.

According to Johnny, one Saturday afternoon the S-4 had surfaced in the path of the Coast Guard destroyer *Paulding* cruising Cape Cod Bay for rumrunners. Rammed by the destroyer just forward of her conning tower, the S-4 sank within five minutes 1,800 yards offshore, entombing forty crewmembers. Most perished instantly, but six remained alive in the forward section for two days or more, tapping out desperate messages in telegraph code on the hull of the sunken vessel, "We are still alive, but not for long." We sat, mesmerized by Johnny's dramatic telling of the story, and stared out into the bay to the very place where the tragedy had occurred in 100 feet of water. Johnny was convinced that government red tape had cost those six men their lives, that they could have been saved if local fishermen had been allowed to salvage the vessel. And there was an even more diabolical suggestion — that the government did not want those men rescued. We had no reason to doubt Johnny. He had been there, he said, as each minute of the tragedy ticked away.

With every retelling of the tale — and I must have heard it a dozen times — my imagination ran farther and farther afield, nourished no doubt by the paranoia of adults who indulged in cold war and JFK assassination conspiracy theories and were convinced that there were spies in our midst. And so it came as a disappointment to learn the truth about the S-4 tragedy — that in the face of deteriorating weather, everything that could have been done to save the crewmen had been done. In 1937, a memorial was dedicated at St. Mary's of the Harbor Church in the east end, and Provincetown has never forgotten those seamen.

Wally Adams, a fisherman who had lost an arm in a fishing accident, came often with stripers that he and Sal scaled, headed, gutted, and cut into fillets and steaks on a small cutting table nailed to the wharf. Propped against an upright, I took in every detail of the operation, watched the knife slide effortlessly through the flesh, watched the flesh lift effortlessly from the long white skeleton. The remains were thrown to the water's edge to waiting, always voracious, seagulls.

Across the summers, from the apartments upstairs and the cottages out on the wharf, Hendrix guitar, Shankar sitar, and melodies from *Jesus Christ Superstar* danced across each new day. The young artists to whom Sal was devoted made their way to the patio, their paraphernalia — easels, paint boxes, and rags — in hand, perfuming the air with turpentine and linseed. They were smells that I drank in deeply, and all these years later, their slightest hint triggers an association with Provincetown. These young painters, who studied with Hensche at the Cape School, worked at the restaurant in the evening, keeping their days free to capture the light and color of Provincetown on canvas. They returned year after year, living a life

meager in material possessions — a few articles of cloth-
ing, a rusted bicycle, a tiny apartment shared with fellow
students — but overflowing with creative inspiration,
intellectual conversation, and the kindness of neighbors.
For the artists at Sal's, their reason for choosing Provincetown was no different than the reason the artists had chosen Provincetown in my grandfather's day. It was, simply,
a place with ample subject matter and a community of
like-minded souls.

For me, as for the artists, Sal's Place was community, an
oasis. Joined by the neighborhood kids, my brothers and I
wove our way in and out of the tableau, tracking sand and
dripping seawater all over the patio and into the restaurant where our forays into the bread drawer and the
refrigerators were, if not encouraged, tolerated. Sal never
objected, never reprimanded, accepting as he did that we,
too — all of us — were part of the life at Sal's. He cared
deeply for young people, whether the artists in whom he
no doubt saw himself a generation earlier, or me or some
other friend's child for whom he was determined to make
the summer stay memorable.

Occasionally I was asked to join the day crew and the
Del Deo family for lunch. By the usual Provincetown
measure, such a lunch was a somewhat formal and lavish
affair as I remember it, with everyone seated in the front
room of the restaurant, the tables covered in bowls of
pasta and soup, plates of fruit, baskets of bread, and bottles of wine. The thrill of being asked to so sumptuous a
meal was surpassed only by the opportunity such an invitation gave me to feast on the banquet of memorabilia
that dressed the walls of that room.

The front room was intimate, more dimly lighted than
the back room, whose wall of plate windows bounced the
light in from the harbor and beach. In the front room two

paned bay windows limited the light filtering in from Commercial Street. Clusters of basketed Chianti bottles and a collection of lights that Sal's father had fashioned from olive oil cans hung from the timbers of the low-slung ceiling. The room, with its simple furniture, crisp linens, and Old World patina, fascinated me. While I ate my lunch, nibbling on olives and tomatoes from an antipasto, twirling spaghetti onto my fork, layering a thick slice of bread with butter, my view flitted from wall to wall.

Over the years, the walls of the front room had become Sal's public scrapbook. They were layered — in some places double- and triple-layered — with posters of Capri and Sorrento, wine-bottle labels, pages from opera libretti, pictures of Caruso, old postcards announcing past season openings of the restaurant, ditties penned by resident writer-waiters, sketches and cartoons done by artist-chefs, exhibition and recital announcements, snapshots of Sal, Jo, Giovanna, Romolo. The edges of posters were curled; the sketches and ditties growing yellow; the photos and postcards perforated by innumerable thumbtacks. Frames were tilted and the photographs inside of them were slipping from their mats.

My favorite photograph was a snapshot of the Beach-combers, a fraternity of artists who had their clubhouse in the east end of town. The picture had been taken sometime in the late 1940s when Sal, still a teenager, had been the Beachcombers' cabin boy, entrusted with cleanup after the Saturday evening communal meal and "meeting." My grand-father, not looking at the camera, was in the back row.

There was no order to the decor, and nothing, I suspect, was ever removed to make room for something new. It was Sal's world: Family. Friends. Italy. Opera. Art.

By late afternoon, tables were being set for the evening's patrons. The day crew would finish up, disheveled, sweaty,

spattered with grease and sauce; the second shift of waiters, busboys, and cooks would arrive, pressed and immaculate. Sal's friends had said their *addios*. A tiny chalkboard in
the front window would announce the dinner selections in
a flowing script — *Manicotti, Bistecca alla Pizzaiola, Pollo del
Giorno, Calamari Stufatii, Vitello Saltimbocca, Pesce di Sta-
gione, Pasta casa linga, Insalata Mista.*

At six, dinner patrons would begin to arrive, flowing
into the narrow alley from all points of the compass,
drawn by the herbal bouquet — thyme, basil, oregano, and
garlic, always the garlic — that wafted from the kitchen. I
would spend most of every evening popping in and out of
the restaurant from my perch out on the wall in front of A
Home at Last, pestering Ernie — Hensche student by day,
salad man by night — or sitting on a stool talking with
Brucie Corea, Joe's son, the dishwasher who madly, and
always with good humor, tamed the avalanche of plates,
pots, and pans that came his way. All evening, ice water
would tumble into glasses, corks pop, steaks and bass siz-
zle, silverware clink, the walk-in door clunk, the espresso
machine whoosh, the fans whir. Faces would glow in buttery candlelight. I might take an early evening walk with a
few friends out on the flats, if the tide was out, or around
the neighborhood. But usually we were there on the wall,
our dangling legs nearly clipped by passing cars and trucks
as their drivers negotiated the narrow passage.

One of the waiters, cooks, busboys was bound to come
out from the restaurant to get something from the store-
room just behind where we sat. We hoped. David, Andrew,
Buzz, Timmy, Freddy, Brizzi, Steve, Peter — they were like
celebrities to us and we waited with girlish eagerness for a
glimpse, for an acknowledgment from these "grownups,"
most of whom were only a few years older than we. For
someone barely into her teens, boys who were eighteen or

twenty were all wisdom and experience, and we were flattered by their attention, imagining it was something it wasn't.

As diners departed, they would leave behind their napkins tossed casually, slices of torn bread in the basket, a last draught of wine in a heavy goblet, a few grapes, cubes of cheese, a slice of melon on the plate — a Chardin still life to me. The dark would settle in around A Home at Last and Sal's Place. The full moon always looked fuller than it did back home. The harbor surface was black except for a silvery runner of moonlight. On moonless nights, the black over Provincetown, far from city glow, was infinite and creamy. The Big Dipper was poised to drink from the harbor, dense crowds of stars trembling like match lights in a deep concert arena. The lighthouse at Long Point shone a steady green; Wood End, an intermittent red. Across the bay the powerful revolving candle at Highland Light, perched atop the steep, eroding clay scarp, punctuated the sky over Truro, reassuring sailors as far as twenty miles out to sea.

Friends, who earlier in the day had been part of the patio mélange, returned in the late evening to share a beer, a glass of wine, Arthur Cohen's home movies, conversation with Sal and anyone else who wanted to be part of the boisterous after-hours conviviality. Long past midnight, as I lay in my bed, my brothers sleeping soundly nearby, I could hear from the restaurant the clang of the trash cans being put out for collection, the din of laughter, the chink of glasses and bottles, the voices — my father's clear tenor among them — raised in inebriated song. The sounds were soporific, a lullaby that rocked me gently to sleep.

Far and Away

FOR THE CREW at Sal's, Monday was the day to catch up on life's ordinary tasks — things like laundry, food shopping, bills, and banking. The restaurant was closed on Mondays, and once the chores were done there was time for a quiet sail in the harbor, for touristy stuff like climbing the monument, time to explore beyond Provincetown, to see Cape attractions that we all had whizzed by on our way to P-Town. Anyone who might be lingering about on the patio as plans were being finalized was welcome to tag along.

For me, the trips out of Provincetown to faraway places up-Cape were the best. The fact that I, then fourteen or fifteen, was allowed to go on these excursions, usually led by young men barely into their twenties, strikes me today as either foolhardy confidence on my mother's part or a courageous letting go of the apron strings. Little did I know that these outings were carefully controlled from behind the scenes. Our parents knew all the players, not difficult in our little neighborhood where intergenerational friendships were the rule and where the same folks returned to the same cottages and apartments year after year. It was an extended family of sorts, and my mother's response would have been altogether different if I had been invited on an up-Cape outing by someone she did not know.

I remember these trips as not having any particular destination. Once out of Provincetown, we abandoned Route 6, preferring to shunpike, turning here, there, up this dirt road, down that narrow lane, bushwhacking, going where few had gone before, ignoring private property signs, exploring, eventually winding up somewhere — Pamet or Corn Hill, Gull Pond, Highland Light, First Encounter Beach. Or Nauset Beach in Orleans. It seems to me that we ended up at Nauset more often than anywhere else.

The Nauset waters on the outer shore of Cape Cod, with their rips and undertow, were unpredictable. The beach dropped off sharply and dangerously. But Nauset had something that we did not have in the calm of Province-town harbor, something that made some of us abandon all caution, all good sense — waves. Big waves, huge waves that surged in from the horizon. The water gathered, heaped, crested, curled, a broken line crashing in sequence, boiling, scampering up onto the beach, glazing, fanning, retreating.

Once we had situated our blankets and towels, we'd all do our own thing. Some brought small surfboards. Others preferred a contemplative stroll along the water's edge. A few would bake in the sun, basting themselves with baby oil (no SPF in those days), turning themselves periodically, basting again, to be sure all parts got evenly roasted.

There was no roasting or roaming for me. I'd spend the afternoon bodysurfing, waiting in the shallows to be picked up by a swell and launched toward shore, sub-merged, groping for a hold, tumbled up onto the beach face in the swash, grasping still for a hold and gasping for a breath as the backwash dragged me, my bathing suit filling with coarse sand and pebbles. I'd just barely recover when another wave would hit me, knocking me prone, face down in the sand.

Over and over and over again the waves would toy with me, as if I were a chunk of flotsam. By afternoon's end I'd be exhausted, my skin tight from the salt and sun, my belly filled with salt water.

Before heading back to P-Town, we'd often stop on the Nauset Road at Mayo's Farm Kitchen to buy tollhouse cookies for the ride home. I remember that on more than one occasion we pooled our change for a box of applesauce squares or macaroons or turnovers, which were presented to our mothers as a peace offering when we arrived home hours overdue.

The ride back to Provincetown always seemed interminable, although it was less than an hour. My skin would be prickly in the hot car, my shoulders and the backs of my legs beginning to burn and redden after having been exposed to the sun all day. We'd almost always stop in Truro, hoping for a glimpse of an osprey on its nest or, better yet, in a thrilling talons-first plunge into the bay for dinner. We'd stop at one of the freshwater kettle ponds to rinse the salt from our bodies and to fly through the air on a rope that swung out over the water. The water would relieve my burning, but only temporarily, and by the time we turned the corner at the old cold storage, I regretted ever having made the trip, a regret that lasted only as long as the sunburn pain. A day or two later I'd be thinking about the next week's outing, hoping it would again be to Nauset. Our parents would be lingering about Sal's Place, always looking a bit anxious until one of them spotted the car and pointed. Though we couldn't hear their words, we just knew that they were saying, "Here they are," and that there was, at that moment, a collective sigh of relief.

I'd immediately fall into a heavy sleep on those Nauset nights. It was a different kind of sleep altogether than the usual drifting off gradually, wallowing in the last few minutes with the pillow contoured just right and the crisp sheet, pulled up under my chin, rising and falling with every breath. On Nauset nights, there was none of that twilight, those last thoughts before sending the day into history. Maybe it was just as well. The sooner I fell asleep, the sooner it would be Tuesday. Sal's Place would be stirring, and I would awake to the sounds and sights and smells I so cherished.

∽ I look back with equal fondness on our annual July blueberry-picking adventure. As much as I would have preferred to trek to the dunes on a Monday morning when I wouldn't miss a single moment at Sal's, nature didn't always cooperate. If the blueberries were ready on a Thursday, on Thursday we went or we risked having the birds beat us to the crop.

Whatever day of the week it was, it always arrived hot. No, more than hot. Scorching. The dunes, we knew before we even got there, would be chokingly oppressive. But we pressed on, a happy troop, players in a Cape Cod tradition. Our parents, grandparents, even great-grandparents had all gone a-blueberrying, leaving their footprints in the soft dune sands.

Arriving in Provincetown for the summer meant abandoning my sneakers to run barefoot for the next few months. Day by day the soft pink bottoms of my feet toughened, the flesh thickened until a ridge of callous encircled the heel and ball. I could endure the hot pavement of the town's narrow streets, the barnacle-encrusted jetties, the pebbly water's edge, even our deck under the midday sun. But my feet were never tough enough for the burnt sand of the dunes, its sharp spears of beach grass and prickly patches of vegetation. Reluctantly, I would stuff my feet back into sneakers before blueberrying, a discomfort added to by the long pants and sleeves that we wore (even more reluctantly) at our parents' insistence to safeguard against poison ivy, scratches, mosquitoes, and of course the fire-breathing sun.

The dunes are a landscape whose music is ethereal — a gentle sibilant wind, a rustle of leaves, sweet, flutelike odes from a rookery — a counterpoint to the thundering percussion of the ocean. But it is more than music that the dunes and sea make together. The dune flora is nourished by the salt spray. The plants thrive, cushions of heather and thickets of fragrant rugosa rose, forests of bonsai sassafras, twisted scrub oak and gnarled pitch pine, stands of spicy bayberry and shrubby beach plum, hummocks of hoary dusty miller, wands of goldenrod, carpets of poison ivy and reindeer lichen, moist cranberry bogs. And, of course, *Vaccinium angustifolium,* the low-bush blueberry.

At one time, the Capescape was tangled in blueberry vines. Now, largely eradicated by commercial development, the blueberries have retreated to where people must make an effort to find them. No doubt this is why the location of a favorite thicket remains, for many of us, our secret. On the Cape Cod of my childhood, there were many secrets. Where the clams had buried themselves was a secret. Where the fish were biting was a secret. And where one's favorite thicket of blueberries was located — that, too, was a secret.

The wild blueberry is a humble berry, not the swollen, robust commercial berry that arrives in our supermarket from Nova Scotia, but a small, firm, delightfully tangy berry whose color is luscious. Picking them, we'd work prodigiously, squinting in the intense sunlight, our foreheads beading with perspiration. We would ease the ready berries into our cupped palms, allowing the berries to cascade into milk or oatmeal cartons. After about an hour's work (it seemed like five), our containers would be filled and our appetites satisfied. We'd draw our names in five-foot letters in the sand, sand so smooth and virgin it was just asking to be written on, then come flushed and panting out of the dune furnace with only one thought — to get to the beach for a swim as quickly as possible, reminded by the parents as we fled to tell no one the whereabouts of our blueberry thicket.

I never had a hand in the making of the various blueberry treats that resulted from our annual morning excursions. One of the mothers who had organized the outing would take possession of the containers and, while we were swimming or boating, transform those humble berries into succulent muffins, breads, and pies that I did have a hand in eating.

Despite the prickly heat, we were a high-spirited group of kids, college students, young artists, and other grownups who turned a simple walk into an adventure, the great dune amphitheater into a classroom. There was always one among us who knew something about botany or geology, someone who picked a leaf or a berry, broke its skin, and offered it up to our noses for a sniff, someone who prattled on about parabolic dunes, foredunes, back-dunes, and furrows, someone who pointed out tiny animal tracks and the five o'clock shadows of magnetite deposits. The artist who encouraged us to not just look, but to see the perfect circles traced in the sand by tips of compass grass twirled in the breeze. And who noted with exuberance the patterns of light and shadow, the big slices of cobalt sky, ochre dune, and green hollow.

All these years later, I still return every July to some of the same patches of blueberries I knew as a kid.

⑥ Rainy days began quietly, like Mondays, and offered an excuse for folks to linger in bed, linger over coffee, over the paper. Sal's visitors still came, but later in the morning, disappearing inside. The tourists eschewed Flyer's, and his orange-and-white dories remained tethered to their moorings gently pitching, lurching, and rolling, collecting the rain like floating cisterns.

As long as there were not too many of them over the course of the summer, rainy days were a welcome respite, even for me. A luminous gray settled over the town, changing one's depth perception, enhancing some colors and shapes while obliterating others. Raindrops stippled the sand, percolated the harbor, dribbled down the windowpanes, and filled the tiny squares of the window screens. A salty freshness rode in on the breeze.

My friends and I turned the rain into another adventure, sloshing through puddles with bare feet, roaming the deserted beach, a landscape of tiny craters, seeing just how wet we could get. The rain was nothing but a nuisance and inconvenience to our parents, who spent the day cooped up playing Scrabble and drinking coffee, mopping up leaks and complaining about how damp the cottage, clothes, and linens would be for the next week. Surrendering to a summer rain is one of those things we leave behind in childhood. Yet the smell of cool rain hitting a hot summer pavement, stirring the dust, is one that for me, all these years later, still triggers memories of our romps.

Downtown, the crowds would swell as the day wore on, vacationers arriving earlier than usual, the weather having scuttled plans for the beach. These visitors had all heard about this place at the end of Cape Cod, this last resort where you could go no farther, heard about its shops, its eateries, its Pilgrim sites, its uninhibited party in the streets. They were eager to see for themselves. Until my later teen years, when the excitement downtown lured me away from the quiet west end, my visits there were few and usually only on rainy days.

We would make our way into town by the beach, splashing at the water's edge, ducking under tottery wharf remnants, sidestepping stranded moon jellies, and climbing over slippery rockweed-draped jetties, reaching Commercial Street along the town landing near the Boatslip Inn & Restaurant. There, we'd merge with the dense pedestrian and bicycle flow that made it nearly impossible for vehicles to pass.

I had my favorite places. First stop, the Shell Shop, at the edge of downtown. I had always loved shells — those bits of perfection, the embodiment of art in science — but I had no familiarity with any but the Atlantic species that were available in ample supply out on the flats in Provincetown harbor. The Shell Shop had exotics from *National Geographic* places like the Maldives, Southeast Asia, Madagascar, places so far away that I wondered if a traveler could even get there. I remember thinking on more than one occasion, as I handled an exquisitely smooth, deliciously pink or yellow specimen, that these shells, heaped in a bin, could not be real. Surely they were fakes, mass-produced for the easily duped, like me, who would pay money for them. And what about those shellacked blowfish and pipefish and sea horses? The large starfish and sea urchins and notched sand dollars? No way could they be real. Though I admired abalone, helmets, and conches, they cost too much. I had several other stops to make and didn't want to spend all my money at the first stop. And they were too big to carry around all afternoon. I would settle happily for the smaller specimens, rummaging through the turbans and sundials, wentletraps, frogs, and murex shells. The only way to get rid of a temptation, said Oscar Wilde, is to yield to it. I did, carefully picking through the bins until I found one or two items whose color and personality suited me that particular day: a coral from Bali, a spiky auger, a Japanese pagoda shell, an olive shell, button shell, or cowrie. I'd hand my money to the clerk and refuse a bag for my acquisition, preferring to fondle it, like a talisman, expecting it to work some magic.

We'd thread through the crowd to Marine Specialties, a surplus store of marine stuff, Army-Navy stuff, and stuff that had no category. A dark cave of a place, one-stop shopping for heavy-knit, dull-green Army sweaters, drinking glasses, fishing bobbers, split-shot sinkers, Army foot powder, pea coats, military rations, Russian collar tabs, folding shovels, glove stretchers, antique printer's type, and canvas ammunition pouches. It was even more unusual in the back rooms, where an old diving bell and life-saving service breeches buoy were suspended from the ceiling, where nets and scallop chain from the old fishing boats were tangled and heaped in piles, and where, from giant clam shells, you expected to see Botticelli's Venus rise. Everything was for sale. It was not known as Provincetown's "Most Unusual Shop" for nothing.

A block or so along Commercial Street, at Adams Pharmacy, we'd spin around on the vinyl-covered stools at the soda fountain waiting for our lime rickeys, vanilla cokes, and frappes. And at The Penney Patch, a penny candy emporium where almost everything did indeed cost a penny, we'd fill straw baskets with Lipsticks, Bull's Eyes, Fireballs, Pixy Stix, Bag-O-Gold, candy cigarettes, Bazooka gum, Lik-m-Aid, and my favorite, candy necklaces that cost a dime. I'd wear that necklace all afternoon, nibbling away first at the yellows, then the whites and the blues, leaving the pinks for last. I never kept a tally as I dropped one piece of candy after another into the basket and, inevitably, had that moment of panic, "What if I don't have enough money?" as the clerk added up my purchase, dropping each piece into a tiny white bag. It was quite surprising, the buying power of twenty-five cents.

We would visit The Rainbow Gallery, a peaceful paint box of color at the end of a yellow-brick walkway where the jewelry, pottery, and stained glass all carried a rainbow motif. The ceiling and walls of the gallery were painted with puffy clouds. The Rainbow Man would dispense colorful little square cards with rainbow designs — rainbow trees, rainbow roads, nighttime rainbows, starlight rainbows — and instruct recipients to put them in their pocket, put them in windows, glue them on letters, decoupage furniture, leave them in restaurants. Visitors were encouraged to write something about rainbows on a large poster board that was provided. Some scribes quoted from Wordsworth, some from the *Wizard of Oz,* and still others wrote original rainbow metaphors: a bridge, a stairway, a mountain, a sign of the hope that can follow despair, the light following the dark, the melding of many into one.

They were the only rainbows we saw on those days when the silver-gray-blue ceiling squeezed down on Provincetown. After our visit with the Rainbow Man, we would make our way across town to climb the Pilgrim Monument, 252 feet of granite that commemorated the Pilgrim's first landing place. In November of 1620, after a perilous two-month voyage aboard the *Mayflower,* the Pilgrims dropped anchor in Provincetown Harbor. After five weeks in that safe haven, during which the Pilgrims explored afield and recorded the first birth and death in the new colony, the *Mayflower* weighed anchor and sailed across Cape Cod Bay to Plymouth. The rest is history, and Provincetown is too often forgotten in the retelling of that history.

Provincetowners, though, never forgot. In 1907, the cornerstone was laid for a Pilgrim monument. President Theodore Roosevelt, arriving in the presidential yacht, attended the ceremony atop Town Hill, and three years later President Taft, also in a yacht and accompanied by the Atlantic Fleet, attended the dedication.

We'd climb the monument a couple of times every summer, and I took delight in relating details of my every ascent to my father, who had been convinced ever since his boyhood that the structure would topple at any minute. "Stay out of that goddamn thing," he'd say, every time. To this day, he has never climbed it.

Sixty ramps and 116 steps, passing by 133 commemorative stones on the way, took us to the top. On a clear day we could see Plymouth. Our eyes glided on, ever curious, across the Atlantic. "We can look all the way to Spain," we used to say. And like looking into the heavens with my telescope, it satisfied the need to explore, to break free, to beachcomb into infinity. No matter if we found nothing. It was enough to just wonder, to be thrilled by the possibilities.

🪢 A rainy, overcast day forced a different perspective, one closer to home. I could see people and cars down below scurrying about. My view followed Commercial Street west to the breakwater, a thin black line separating the harbor from the salt marsh. My eyes followed the flat spiral of sand out to Long Point, where the squat little lighthouse seemed to glow behind the gray. Looking east through the mist to Truro, my eyes followed the curve of creamy-colored dunes, punctuated by Shankpainter and Clapp's ponds, north and west around to Race Point. The world below was reduced to its essential shapes, a modernist painting, in gauzy greens, reds, blues, and yellows, of parallelogram rooftops, triangle steeples, square ponds, round treetops, elliptical dunes, rectangular wharves and streets. Out in the harbor, looking south, boats shuttled about. Town Wharf, straight and strong, jutted into the harbor, surrounded at its end by a cluster of fishing boats off-loading their catch.

We'd race back down the ramps, dizzy from the spiraling descent. Making our way back home, though in no hurry, we'd stop at the head of the wharf for a foot-long hot dog at John's. Moments later we'd be watching the fishermen in their yellow oils, buckets dripping water and dropping fish as they were hoisted from deep within the hold up onto the wharf. The fish were belched onto tables, sorted, packed, iced, and loaded into waiting trucks. The seagulls were always frantic, the air ripe, the tourists fascinated, the fishermen oblivious to all the attention, or at least pretending to be so.

As those rainy afternoons drew to a close, everyone — including me, who always loved the kitsch that Provincetown did so well — would be trying to leave town at the same time with salt-water taffy and souvenirs of Provincetown. We'd make one last stop at Café Poyant for a hot chocolate heaped with fresh whipped cream and then head home.

I'd lie in my bed, the sheets cool and slightly damp, the last of my penny candy tucked in beside me, my shells turning over in my fingers. The raindrops on the roof would sound like drumbeats calling me to some far-off place. And as I'd travel there, the doleful song from the foghorn out in the bay would float in on a stiffening sea breeze that heaved the sheer curtains in my little room.

⑥ Later in the summer, weeks after nature had provided us with blueberries, we had a second opportunity to put our hunter-gatherer skills to the test when it came time for the clambake, a communal banquet that, perhaps more than anything else, was testimony to the munificence of the sea. Except for the cobbed corn, our food came from the harbor, where no license, permit, or even permission was needed.

I was a member of the team dispatched to the far west end, to the mile-long riprap breakwater that stretched across the harbor from the Provincetown Inn to Long Point. Our job was to gather mussels, the smooth blue mussels that anchored themselves by threads to the granite rocks. If the tide was out, my companions and I would make our way across the harbor flats to the breakwater, selecting a spot far enough out where there was good tidal flow, where the mussels spent the better part of each day submerged. Not only were these mussels more robust, but the washing tides inhibited toxins from invading the orange flesh.

While walking across the flats, the ball of my foot might happen upon a quahog — never call them simply clams — just beneath the surface, and with a flick of the toes, I could tumble the thick, tight-shelled specimen up onto the sand. Though we were not expected to bring back quahogs, we tossed them into our bucket anyway, knowing full well that there would always be room in the pit for a few more. We knew them by various names — cherrystones, littlenecks, or chowder clams — depending on their size. They had been prized by Native Americans of the Wampanoag tribe, who found their flesh a gustatory delight and polished their purple-stained shell interiors into beads that were used in barter. Modern P-Town natives as well as washashores prize them, too, gathering and eating them by the bucket and always in search of the perfect purple.

If there was little challenge in capturing the quahog, capturing the elusive razor clam — what we knew as a jackknife clam — proved to be the ultimate clamming challenge. A depression in the sand flat with a hole in its middle gave the clam away. I knew it was there, standing upright close to the surface in its slightly bowed shells. If you didn't get to it within two scoops of sand, it was gone, retreating deep into the sand and out of reach. Despite my well-conceived plan of attack, I was always frustrated in my attempts to capture one of these fast diggers. An old-timer once told me that razor clams can feel the vibration of footsteps on the sand and that they hunker down, laughing at you even before you start digging. I've since heard the same theory from naturalists, who try hard not to let folklore get the better of them, so it must be true. As for my digging, I always did come up empty-handed and had to settle instead for the empty shells, occasionally an intact hinged pair, that were scattered about the flats. To this day I have never unearthed a live one.

Mussel gathering fell somewhere between quahog gathering and razor clamming on the difficulty scale. Finding them was a cinch. There was no shortage of the dense clusters. Removing them was another story. Once we were in position, we would plunge our hands deep into the rock recesses past the barnacles, periwinkles, dogwinkles, starfish, anemones, and bladderweed that shared the breakwater. With a death grip on a cluster, I'd rip the mussels from their habitat. My fingernails would break, and the tips of my fingers would become crisscrossed with tiny lacerations from the barnacles that encrusted both the mussels and the rocks. Occasionally a crab, lurking in the rocks and disturbed by my reach, would scamper across my hand, scaring the bejesus out of me. My arm would recoil, my elbow banging against the rock and sending a spasm through my body. My shriek never failed to elicit a comment from someone in the group that crabs, even those scurrying across your hand in the dark bowels of the jetty, were preferable to a broad-daylight encounter with the rats that also lived there.

I'd heard about the breakwater rats, described as robust gnawing mammals, and although rodents such as voles and muskrats did, in fact, secret themselves away in the adjacent marsh, I never did determine whether the breakwater rats were these same voles and muskrats just out for a stroll or whether they were another animal altogether. They were certainly made out to be some sort of mutant creature. I had never seen one and hoped never to see one. Still, as I went about my harvesting, thoughts of the rats stayed with me — the stories *could* be true, I told myself — and I am certain that had I actually met up with a saltwater-drenched rodent, my days of gathering mussels would have come to an immediate end. I would have insisted on quahog duty or demanded to be counted out.

If the tide was up, we'd walk to the breakwater along the water's edge, climb up onto the rocks at the Provincetown Inn, and make our way out across the smooth, flat faces of granite, pooled with sun-dried salt, the gaps between the rocks laced by delicate, perfect spiderwebs. Along the way, we would encounter a breakwater community made up of coiled lovers, fathers and sons fishing for pogies, topless sunbathers, skinny-dippers, readers, pot smokers, and solitaries in meditative trances.

It was so much easier to gather mussels at low tide, standing on the flats, than at high tide when we had to wedge ourselves and our buckets in the rocks or lie on our bellies, curl over, and reach in, the blood rushing and thumping into our brains. Whatever the tide, we would make our quota quickly from the jetty's bounty, take a dip in the old swimming hole, bask on the sun-warmed rocks, and return to the beach between Sal's and Flyer's, where a pit had been dug in the sand, well above the high-water mark.

My work was not yet complete. There was cleaning to be done, a tedious process of scraping and scrubbing the teardrop-shaped mussels free of barnacles, limpets, and holdfast, rinsing, scraping again, the blue-black-purple shells drying to a dusky twilight hue. As I cleaned, it occurred to me that shells, like pebbles, are best appreciated when first plucked from the water, when their surfaces glisten and all of their hues are accentuated. I often gathered shells, especially the colorful bay scallop shells, only to find their tints quite dull once the shell had dried. My father had shown me how to lick the shell or stone to restore its pinks and oranges, its purples and yellows, the contrast in the scallop's flutes, the speckles on the pebble. Perhaps, like the moon snail's delicate sand collar that fell apart after being removed from the water, the dulling of the shells and pebbles was an act of preservation, nature's way of discouraging the predator, of saying, "See, I'm not very interesting. Throw me back."

One after another I'd toss my mussels into a bucket of water to flush out any stray grains of sand, though no one ever seemed to mind a few grains of sand in the meal. The other gatherers would return with their fruits of the sea — cherrystones, steamers, lobsters, and bladder weed. Corn and butter would arrive from the A&P. Someone would bring the large stones (saved summer to summer) that went first into the sand pit, lining its bottom. Chunks of driftwood, gathered from the beach over the previous weeks, were stacked on top of the stones and set afire, allowed to burn, fueled with more wood, allowed to burn until reduced to embers, until the stones were red with heat. It would take several hours. Only then could the cooking begin.

The shellfish — steamers, quahogs, and mussels — were bundled in dozens of foil packets. The corn, still in its husks, was also wrapped in foil. Lobsters were set aside in buckets of water. A bed of seaweed, each bladder pregnant with seawater, was laid on the rocks, on top of which were spread the ears of corn looking like missiles in their silver sleeves. Next came another layer of seaweed, and on it went the packets of shellfish. More layers. Lobsters tossed in, struggling, tangling in the seaweed. More seaweed on top, filling the pit. Finally, a broad piece of wet canvas was stretched across the opening, anchored on the beach around its edges, and then covered with an impenetrable lid of sand under which our feast would bake.

The bladders of the seaweed would heat to bursting, their saltwater dribbling down to the bottom of the pit, to the rocks where it would be turned to steam. Shellfish would open, spewing and commingling their broth in the foil packets; lobsters would writhe, transforming during their slow death from purple-black to brilliant red; kernels of corn would soften on the cob.

The meal, hidden from sight, would cook all afternoon, guarded by adults who had arrived in the late morning and arranged their blankets and umbrellas, their books and sketch pads. They'd gab and gossip and drink cocktails, shifting their beach chairs to follow the sun as it rode across the afternoon sky. Folks would come and go. The tide would work its way up the beach and back down again. We'd swim, or tool about the harbor in boats, or scamper back and forth to one another's cottages, across the street to the O'Donnells' or to Perry's Market, down the street to the Everetts' place or to the Germains' house. After four or five hours someone would make the decision to peel back the canvas and inspect the food. The aromas would be released skyward from the pit in a blast of heat. Word would spread quickly that the chow was ready, and folks young and old would filter down to the beach.

I'd eat three or four ears of corn drenched in butter, savoring them as everyone else did the steamers or mussels saturated in broth. Lobster meat, removed from the claw and drowned in melted butter, was devoured with a gustatory swoon I have seen only among lobster eaters. For me, those clambakes weren't as much about the food as about the gathering, being part of the continuum, carrying on in much the same way as my parents had twenty years earlier and their parents had a generation before that. They were about becoming one with the elements, the air, the water, the earth, and the fire, and for a snippet of time, existing in a primitive state.

As the new moon darkness draped over us, the orangey-blue bonfire on the beach danced and licked and snapped, tossing a confetti of embers skyward and playing on the faces of dinner guests. There was singing and conversation. I'd fall back into the cool sand and stare at the Milky Way. What I saw was the past, not the stars as they were at that moment, but as they had been so very long ago. I wondered if they were still out there, somewhere behind their afterglow.

Souvenirs

DURING MY CHILDHOOD in Provincetown there were
events — and every summer had them — that never quite
repeated themselves in the same way, events that became,
like my shells and starfish and bits of driftwood, souvenirs
to take home.

It might be an August night when the sky rippled in
waves of blue and gold. I waited the next evening, at the
same time, in the same place, assuming the curtains of
color would return. They didn't and I wished I had paid
closer attention. Or witnessing an approaching front, dark
and ominous, with a brief squall of pearl drops that sent
everyone running for cover, after which God's paintbrush
splashed a rainbow on the afternoon. Or the moment
when the clouds opened just enough for a column of sunlight to join heaven to harbor. There were midnight swims
— the polished, black marble water pulled in higher than
its normal height by a full moon — when we joined the
crew from Sal's to dive and jump off the apartments on the
wharf. And then, too, there were nights when schools of
stripers, chasing feed, wove in and out around the pilings,
in knee-deep water, right under our noses.

There was that evening in 1969 when man first walked
on the moon. There would be other moon landings and
walks, but none would have the same magic as that night
in July. There had been weeks of anticipation, then days,
then mere hours, and finally moments that seemed as long
as the previous weeks. For more than 24 hours we crowded

around a tiny black-and-white television, watching images that gripped our imagination beamed from a quarter of a million miles away. Throughout the day, friends came and went. In the evening, the crew from Sal's, in between serving meals, busing tables, broiling bass, and steaming steamers, were in and out of our cottage. "Have they landed yet?" "Have they opened the hatch yet?" Little else that night seemed very important. In that crowded cottage at the tip of Cape Cod, we counted ourselves among the 600-million-strong fellowship witnessing that extraordinary marriage of art, which appeals to what Joseph Conrad called the "capacity for delight and wonder," and science.

For me, it was also a time of discovery. Endless possibility and discovery. That summer, and the next few summers, I volunteered as an usher at the Provincetown Playhouse on the Wharf, getting my first taste of O'Neill, Williams, Pinter, Simon, and Albee in the company of some 200 theatergoers who sat on wooden, cushioned pews and barrels in a cramped fish shack, tucked away on a beach downtown. I was too young then to understand the themes of guilt, denial, recrimination, the compulsions and complexities of the human condition. I did, though, respond to the magic of the theater, that a stage could be set with the simplest of props, that a curtain could be pulled back, and that I could be transported from my life into another world.

The world I always returned to was that of the sea. I was nourished by its surprises — in the harbor, a pod of porpoise mimicking breaking wavelets, a lone shark cruising sluggishly to and fro in search of mackerel, butterfish and flounder, a beach robed in moon jellies, a blackfish roaming in the shallows only yards away from me as I canvassed the sea floor in waist-deep water for sand collars. And the school of bluefish, formidable opponents of fishermen, vicious predators of mackerel and herring, that burst the harbor surface.

I remember the calm harbor of one afternoon shattered by a "wolf pack" of blues chasing feed fish. About a hundred yards offshore, the bloodthirsty school ripped, slashed, exploded in a frenzy of feeding. Though it lasted only minutes, the attack churned the harbor from blue to white water until the fish left as quickly as they had come.

∞ If such small events defined the harbor for me, it was the bigness of nature that defined Race Point. Commercial Street ends at the Provincetown Inn. There, the road joins the Province Lands Road, which winds around the salt marsh, out to Herring Cove Beach, what the locals called New Beach, continuing on to Race Point about four miles from Sal's. A cold-water body fed by the frigid Labrador Current, here was the Great Beach about which Thoreau had written a century earlier. Cut away by murderous winter storms, rebuilt by summer surf, year after year, life cannot hold on here the way it can in the harbor. There are few souvenirs: deadman's fingers, egg cases, vertebrae, sea-wash balls, pebbles. But it is not to beachcomb that people come to Race Point. Rather, they come still, as I did so many years ago, to stare across the wilderness to a soothing horizon, to fill themselves with the vastness, to listen to the ocean's great curls of water, marbleized with spume, pounding on the shore. The air was different out there, fuller, freer, gathering its vigor from unfettered travels across the Atlantic.

We made a handful of pilgrimages to Race Point each summer. In the earlier years, it was usually Mrs. O'Donnell who packed up the car with blankets, an umbrella, something to drink, Lobo playing on the transistor radio, and took us there. As we grew older, with our newfound independence, we hitchhiked. We could do that without worry back then, jumping onto a tailgate or into the back of a pickup. Or we rode our bikes.

I remember one hot day taking the bike trail that meandered through the dunes and moorlands. It was by no means an easy ride, through oppressive air that was roiled by ribbons of heat emanating from the sand. The sun beat down on us, and for me, who had never cared for hat and sunglasses, it felt as though my hair was aflame and that my face would crack from tightness at any moment. We turned the ride into a contest of sorts, jockeying for the lead on our bikes, feeling the ache in our knees on our ascents, the exhilaration of tucking in on the descent, seeing whose momentum could carry them farthest without peddling.

At Race Point, we chained our bikes to the rack and raced, flush-faced and panting, with our last burst of energy across several hundred yards of scorching, slipping, swallowing sand to the water's edge where we threw down our towels, tore off our T-shirts, and launched ourselves into the nippy water.

Offshore, the treacherous, unforgiving Peaked Hill shoals lay in wait under a heaping sea that had claimed so many sailing vessels and lives over the years. Nestled in the dunes behind the beach were dilapidated shacks, a reminder of the Peaked Hill Bars Lifesaving Station, one of the nine original shore stations spread out along the Great Beach from Provincetown to Monomoy, off Chatham, built to assist shipwrecked sailors.

The surfmen, "guardians of the ocean graveyard," patrolled the lonely, battered beach with their lanterns and red warning rockets during the storm season from August to May. They built the dune shacks without government authorization to accommodate their families who visited the outpost on weekends. After the Peaked Hill Station was abandoned in the 1920s, the squatters' shacks were sold to artists and writers. These were spare dwellings, made homey with tiny cots, writing tables, kerosene lanterns and stoves, a coffeepot, a few cups and dishes, and driftwood shelves filled with Plato, Shakespeare, and Milton. The shacks were buffeted by gales, pelted by rain, closeted by darkness and fog, and piled under by drifting sand and snow. Eugene O'Neill, Jack Kerouac, Norman Mailer, Harry Kemp, and Edmund Wilson, among others, found spiritual nourishment, artistic inspiration in the solitude, in the starkness, in a bird's cry, the wind's howl, in nature's often violent beauty.

We didn't stay long, just long enough to rest and cool off. We watched the gulls working the thick wrack, missing nothing, back and forth, edge to edge, making contact with everything, devouring the succulent tidbits. Plucking out a starfish. Searching for an embryo in a mermaid's purse or an egg case. Snatching a crab, gripping it with a crunch, and sending it down the gullet whole.

Our bike ride back to the west end was more leisurely. We pedaled, brakes squealing whenever someone had picked up a bit too much speed to negotiate the twists and turns in the bike trail. We were always aware of the vagrant sand on the paved trail that could, at any moment, send our tires out from under us.

At New Beach we emerged from the hushed dunes and moors, zigging and zagging our way across the parking lot and out onto the road, zigging and zagging between the broken white lines down the middle of the road, side to side in flowing hairpin turns. We pedaled, building up speed, to the place where the road began its descent around the salt marsh. And it was there in the hollow of the road, in a cool pocket under splayed treetops, that I feasted on wild sand rose and salt air, pine and privet, the flavors delicate and balanced, garnished with dune dust. I sped through it wanting desperately to stop and prolong the experience, but my companions were already rounding the next bend. I revisited the spot the next day hoping to experience the sensation again. The rugosa rose was pungent, but I could not detect the other fragrances.

Rosa rugosa, known in the area simply as the wild sand rose, is a perfect emblem, it seems to me, of the old Provincetowners themselves: unassuming, idiosyncratic, informal of habit, adaptable, and vigorous. It's a primitive rose, natural, that thrives in salt spray.

During my childhood the wild sand rose scrambled luxuriantly across the dunes and skirted the shore, providing a superb display of color, cheerful faces of crepelike, five-petal carmine and white blooms tossing against a blue backdrop of ocean and sky. Its tangle of puncturing stems deterred all but the most determined from trampling on it, while at the same time helping to anchor and consolidate the ever-shifting sand.

I could never get enough of the wild rose and was especially delighted when it would waylay me by escaping from a neighborhood garden and assaulting me on my evening walk. I would stop to plunge my nose in its flower, holding it by its hip, still just a small green swelling that, over the course of the summer, would grow to cherry-tomato size and turn scarlet.

ⓖ In the space between the far edge of day and the near edge of night, I enjoyed just roaming about the grid of neighborhood near Sal's, drifting as through a tidal creek, into the tributaries — up Mechanic Street, over Tremont, down Cottage, up Nickerson, down Soper, up West Vine. What impressed me most on these strolls was the town's casual character, the quiet rejection of discipline, the unwillingness to conform. No two houses were alike, no two gardens, no two front doors, no two fences. And yet there was room for them all and they all belonged. There were houses finished with shingles, others clapboarded. A simple, unadorned picket fence edged one yard, a chain-link fence another. Another neighbor's parcel was barely visible behind a dense thicket of rose or an impenetrable screen of shiny green privet. Somewhere around the Fourth of July, clusters of white privet flowers would open and the hedge would release its heavy sweetness — provided that the owner had not taken the clippers to it in late spring. Its first exhalation of the summer was the most satisfying, and as with the wild rose, I never tired of encountering it in my travels. I wait for it now in my own yard, in those first days of July, and its fragrance and effect are unchanged from what they were then. I'm always brought back to one particular spot on Nickerson Street.

There was a house with a manicured lawn and, next door, a front yard given over to a riot of delphinium, larkspur, phlox, hydrangea, bee balm, glads, dahlias, and double hollyhocks, all in glorious blossom. There was evidence everywhere I looked in Provincetown that the muses had visited — seashells and pebbles embedded in walkways, old skiffs planted with petunias and nasturtium, houses trimmed in pink and turquoise, arbors made of ship's timbers, window boxes painted with sea nymphs, a whaler's harpoon lashed above a door, handmade ceramic house numbers, driftwood garden ornaments — and confirmation that most people have in them the need to be creative.

❧ Next to the West End Racing Club an open, meticulously tended grassy lot provided nourishment for the spiritually hungry, who sat in thoughtful meditation on the seawall, staring across the harbor. Perry's Market, perched on the easterly edge of the grass, offered another kind of nourishment. From my earliest years, I can remember being dispatched by my mother to Perry's for milk or bread and by my father for cigarettes, clutching a scribbled note authorizing the sale. The proprietor, Johnny O'Donnell, had bought the store sometime during the 1960s from Bert Perry, for whom he had worked as a clerk. A kindly, avuncular man probably in his fifties, I remember Mr. O'Donnell always wearing a white apron. When I was just into my teens, he often let me load up the soda machine out front or fill the metal newspaper rack with the Boston and New York papers and, of course, the local paper, the *Advocate*, which was eagerly awaited each Thursday for its pleasant columns by John Bell musing in "Alongshore," Heaton Vorse in "Southwind," and Howard Mitcham cooking up a storm in "Cape Tip Gourmet." There were also wind charts, airport notes, softball-league standings, and yacht club race results. Most of the time I sold out my stack of papers to passersby, at twenty-five cents apiece, before I even got them into the rack.

We were in and out of Perry's a dozen times a day, always in dripping bathing suits and with sandy feet, manhandling the merchandise and letting precious cold air escape from the freezer chests while we stood there trying to decide whether we were in the mood for an ice-cream sandwich or an Eskimo Pie. But Mr. O'Donnell, like Sal, never scolded, never seemed the least bit annoyed by our appalling lack of consideration.

A pleasant ripe fruit ether trickled out of Perry's, off the stoop and into the street, whose tar patches were always soft under the summer sun. The plate-glass windows were plastered with notices and posters, and one poster in particular always caught my eye. I waited for it, hoping every day, as summer wore on, to see it, the one with the bold Gauguin colors, the irresistible reds, blues, yellows, and greens, the one that announced that the Carnival was coming to town.

⑥ For a handful of days each summer, a fallow field on the outskirts of town along Route 6 became a surreal shrine of blinking, oscillating, and flashing colored bulbs, whirring generators, bells, sirens, whistles, fluttering pennants. The ghostly glow on the horizon at dusk summoned the fairgoers. They flowed out of the downtown, up Bradford Street, following the glow through the parking lots and out to Shankpainter Road, where they came under the spell of sentimental songs from the Wurlitzer, raucous rock and roll from the adrenaline rides, swirling fragrances from fried foods and sweets.

All around us were the energies: sliding, gliding, flying, rolling, spinning, shaking, snaking, cascading. With our long strips of tickets accordioned in our palms, we would move from one amusement to the next, riding the Ferris wheel, the cups and saucers, the Zipper, the Tilt-A-Whirl, the Caterpillar and bumper cars, the giant slide and the merry-go-round. Our intestines would flip-flop, our brains rattle in our skulls, our faces contort, eyes watering, mouths drooling, hair flying, limbs going limp. We couldn't get enough.

We'd roam around with syrupy sno-cones, greasy fried dough, dribbling ice cream, and velvety penuche. The games' vendors would stand like courtesans in their booths, fringed with big, plush, beribboned, glass-eyed lions, cats, dogs, monkeys, and bears. They'd solicit us, those purveyors of pleasure, playing a confidence game. "How about it, test yourself. You're looking like a winner."

"Hey, bet you're feeling lucky tonight." "For you, only twenty-five cents a game." "No losers." We'd throw darts at balloons, toss rings around blocks of wood, shoot baskets, pluck plastic ducks from a bath, squirt water guns at targets, and bowl balls up a ramp, all the while eyeing the prizes overhead and on the walls inside. The vendors were right about one thing — there were no losers, but it was rare that anyone took home the prizes that had tempted us. More often than not our reward was a plastic bauble or a small, badly stitched stuffed animal with pasted-on paper eyes.

Still, we'd return the next night and the next and the next, every night under the spell, until the Carnival left town. For a few days more, the red and blue and yellow and green poster, sun-faded, would hang in the window at Perry's. One day, it would be gone, its place taken by a silk-screened poster announcing a piano recital or a hand-printed flyer describing a lost kitten.

☞ As I walked around the neighborhood, I would take the slightest greeting from someone on a porch or stoop as an invitation to stop and chat. It was mostly the older native-born Provincetowners in those days, in those homes, on those front steps, people full of wistful remembrances of the town that they knew was changing faster over the course of months than it had over decades. I would never tire of their talk, waiting while they dropped their hook and line deep into their memories and tried to figure just how so-and-so came to be related to so-and-so. "Her father was married to so-and-so's first wife's sister. I think." Or they would gesture across the street. "Did you know that right over there, that used to be a. . . ." They talked to me about winter blizzards and the time the harbor froze over. They remembered Commercial Street when it had been lined with elms and lighted by oil lamps. Talked about boiling up periwinkles in tin cans over a fire on the beach and picking the meat out of the shell with small sticks. Remembered Charles Hawthorne, dressed all in white flannel, painting for his class on the beach. Remembered the tar pots in the fields out on the other side of town, the smell of tar all over town, the dipped fishing nets spread out on the grass to dry. Remembered unpaved side roads, rumrunners, coal barges, visits by fleets of navy warships and sailing ships, Teddy Roosevelt's visit, the artists' annual costume ball, the 1898 storm that piled the inner beach with pieces of the fishing fleet and the outer beach of Cape Cod with bodies washed ashore off the vessel *Portland.*

If you didn't have time to stop, to talk, if you needed to be somewhere, you didn't roam the neighborhood because as sure as Joe Corea would be sitting on his fence, you'd be late for wherever it was you were going. People's lives were fluid, open to the lingering moment rather than held hostage by a schedule, by appointments. I'd find myself leaning against a fence for hours, dinner smells reaching out to grab me, screen doors whining open, clapping shut, someone's piano sonata tickling my ear, someone else's Puccini soothing my heart.

I remember one evening when the side streets fell first into night's deepening shadow as the sun set. The open harbor continued to glow for a few minutes more, in the remains of the day. I continued on, taking the circuitous route, closing my eyes and feeling the undulations of the streets underfoot. I made my way to the Dairy Queen and bought myself a spiraled soft ice-cream cone dipped in chocolate. I strolled down West Vine, turning the cone round and round against my tongue to catch the drips, turned onto Tremont, buzzing, whining, and trilling with night insects, and crossed over the dark, empty corridors of Soper and Nickerson. From the crest of Nickerson, my eyes looked down the slope, distracted momentarily by the twinkle of a firefly, beyond the grassy lot next to Perry's, across the harbor to where a fat, slightly flattened, ruddy moon rose from behind Truro. Once such a moon was anathema to the mooncussers, salvagers who (legend told) prowled the outer beach in the dark of a moonless night, showing lights that unsuspecting offshore vessels took to be beacons of safety. Captains steered their ships on what they thought was a course clear of danger, only to find themselves hopelessly floundering on the shoals, pulverized by cruel water. Their cargoes, cast ashore, were claimed by looters who cussed a moonlit night because it illuminated the shore and interfered with their nefarious business.

I watched as the full moon ascended, shedding its pink, rolling out its long boardwalk of light across the harbor, connecting it with me. I followed, under the moon's spell, down Nickerson, across Commercial Street, stepping over the black chain edging the lot, sliding my toes through cool, dewy blades of grass, and settling on the seawall, my legs dangling over the side. The beach below was completely covered by a spring tide whose pulsing thumped rhythmically against the base of the wall. I watched the moon climb, and by the time I had finished my ice cream, it was stark silver-white, promising that tomorrow would be as handsome a day as the one that was taking its last breath.

West End Racing Club

IN THE EARLY SEVENTIES, when I was fourteen or
fifteen, we left A Home at Last and moved a few doors
west on Commercial Street to a cottage behind the Oldest
House. I recall only vaguely the layout of the cottage,
which was just across the street from the West End Racing
Club. Like A Home at Last, the place was rustic, the sand
from so many previous tenants wedged between the
creaky floorboards. Unlike A Home at Last, it was not on
the water. Although we could see the harbor, it was not
that unencumbered view I had cherished for so many
years. We were sandwiched by Soper Street on one side
and on the other by a grassy footpath, one of Provincetown's old byways, the still-visible ruts worn by old fish
carts white with crushed quahog shells.

The move to the Oldest House was more an emotional
leap than a physical one. Not being part of the day-to-day
life of Sal's, I never again felt really at home there. I never
swam at the beach there again, but every time I strolled
down the street I craned to see what was going on, who
was there on the patio. Life seemed to carry on as I had so
fondly remembered, many of the same faces coming and
going, the young artists readying their easels and paint
boxes for the day, their paint rags strung out on a
makeshift laundry line down on the beach.

The Italian aromas still trickled out; the reel-to-reel
played opera, Giovanna and Romolo went about their
chores, and Tommy DeCarlo and his mother, Sibylle, took

their morning swims. My parents still rendezvoused with friends on the patio, and those times were my chance to reenter that world under the pretense of asking my mother or father for money or to tell them where I might be going, to feel again the perfection that I had felt when we lived at A Home at Last. They were moments I cherished, but moments tinged with sadness as well as something else, something I did not understand until much later. I remember at times feeling an utter disdain for what I saw as the dull routine and repetition of the lives here. How could they keep doing the same thing day after day, talking to the same people day after day, about the same things, day after day? Rather than admit that something profoundly special had passed from my life, I chose to annihilate it.

That first summer away from Sal's was the hardest as I tried to cling to the familiar but was excited by the new. We were exploring farther afield, riding our bikes all the way to Truro or boating way out beyond the Point into the bay. We went regularly to the Provincetown Inn at the far end of town for a swim in the pool, taking great pleasure in eluding the front desk clerk and passing ourselves off to the pool attendant as guests of the hotel. Unlike many of my friends who cringed at the thought of sharing the ocean with all sorts of slippery, tickling, bug-eyed creatures, I loved the harbor and never cared much for pools (still don't). My sole interest was its diving board. And it was a good one, with plenty of spring. I might have become a stronger swimmer if the sense of being catapulted through the air had not been so exhilarating.

One summer, the older O'Donnell girls, then college students, had their own cottage up on Tremont Street only a block or two away from their parents on Mechanic Street — though it might as well have been miles. All types of young people congregated there, coming and going at all hours of the day and night. Friends from home, friends of friends from home, college roommates just back from some far-flung corner of the globe. They got sick on red wine. They had boyfriend and girlfriend troubles. They kissed and told. They brought back stories of downtown after dark, of Fellini and Allen and Bergman movies at the New Art Cinema, of cappuccinos and mocha frosteds at Poyant's, of dancing the night away at gay bars, of men dressed as women, women dressed as men. For me, four or five years younger and infinitely less sophisticated, it was all quite tantalizing.

My home away from home became the West End Racing Club. The club, as everyone called it, was not what you think of when someone says yacht club. This was a community club that welcomed anyone who had the five-dollar membership fee and who pledged to abide by the Code of Ethics.

Hundreds of children, local kids as well as summer visitors, learned how to sail Sunfish, Robins, and Blue Jays in an atmosphere of cooperation and good fun. Many of the club's members sailed in weekend races — of Sunfish, catamarans, Lightnings, and open-class boats — sponsored by the "other" yacht club in town, the Provincetown Yacht Club in the east end. I had always watched these races from Sal's patio because Flyer and his sons, Grassie and Jimmy, and Donald Thibeault, who worked for Flyer, were among those competing. On a couple of occasions Jimmy, who was never anything but kind and generous to me even though I was considerably younger, invited me to go along as crew on Flyer's pride and joy — his green-hulled wooden sloop Columbia, every inch of which he had built with his own hands.

Every day, summer after summer after summer of my childhood, Columbia sat comfortably out in the harbor, beyond Flyer's fleet of outboards, the matriarch of the fleet, tugging at her mooring. I had long admired her pure design from afar and for years could only imagine the thrill of being onboard during a race, her large mainsail and jib ready to burst with breeze. Or in a fairer wind she'd fly her spinnaker, slashed with bold color, and what a sight that would be to behold. When my first chance to be aboard during a race came one morning, I could hardly contain my excitement, but at the risk of being replaced by someone more experienced, I did not dare to admit that I hadn't a clue how to sail. It didn't matter, though. There was only one captain on board. The rest of us did exactly as we were told.

Those experiences, and a few other casual sails in the harbor with folks staying on Sal's wharf, helped pique my interest in sailing and in joining the West End Racing Club. For years I had seen the kids going in and out through the club's double doors with such purpose and enthusiasm. From Sal's we could see them rigging the boats on the beach, bailing them, fixing this and that, could hear them talking that distinctive, peculiar, poetic sailor's lingo — luffs and jibes and battens — that was as foreign to me as Portuguese. All the while I was thinking it was something I'd like to be a part of.

While we were still living at A Home at Last, I finally did join the club — I was 13 or 14 — and regretted that I hadn't joined sooner because sixteen was the cutoff for membership. As it turned out, I remained a member until I was twenty. I never knew if they had relaxed the rules for me or if I was the oddball, the only kid who wanted to be associated with the place, surrounded by mostly preteens, when others my age were enjoying far more worldly adventures.

I made new friends at the club. For so long my circle had been only the children of my parent's friends, but now I was meeting local kids, Portuguese kids, kids whose fathers were fishermen or plumbers or cemetery workers, kids who introduced me to a Provincetown that I would not have known otherwise — the short cuts, the vast tracts of woods behind Route 6 scarred with fire roads and dotted with ponds, and the remote edges of the outer beach where a culture had grown up among the surf fishermen whose jeeps huddled at the high-water mark. My father cringed to hear their names, resuscitating the Yankee-Portuguese bigotries of his childhood. "Stay the hell away from them," he'd say to me, as his father had said to him, as if by association I demeaned myself and the family. His words seemed quaint and halfhearted, and I ignored them.

My memories of the West End Racing Club are every bit as fond as my memories of Sal's. Our Skipper was Tommy Dahill, a townie whose father was a schoolteacher. Tommy was a strong, handsome kid, a year or two older than I, although he seemed even older, perhaps because of his responsibility. He was a natural at running the club, handy when it came to fixing things, comfortable with all the kids, a superb swimmer and sailor. Like Flyer's son, Arthur Joe, Tommy had been born to the water. I have often thought that both should have taken their sailing skills aboard an America's Cup yacht or to Newport, where they would have been appreciated and rewarded. Both stayed in Provincetown.

The club was open weekdays from nine until noon and one to four. The sight of the double doors propped open stirred in me the same kind of anticipation I had felt when Sal threw open the doors each morning. The harbor out beyond the old cold-storage wharf sparkled in the morning sun. The club's beach, caressed by the overnight tide, was smooth, the sand cool, the last push of the tide marked by a scarf of bladder weed, skeins of eelgrass, pebbles, and periwinkles. The neighbors to the west trickled out onto their decks with coffee and newspaper. Laundry was hung out. Garden sprinklers filled yards with snippets of rainbows. Hedge trimmers buzzed. Freshly cut grass released a cool, sweet moisture that I could smell up and down Commercial Street.

If the tide was in — and we all carried the tide chart in our heads — and the weather was good, Tommy would be out at the moorings first thing, gathering the Sunfish and towing the cluster of white hulls to the beach where they would wait to be rigged. The deck at the club filled early with browned youngsters with local names like Silva and Roderick, Medeiros and Costa who scrambled to get sails, centerboards, and rudders. Billy and Nancy Gilman and Lisa and Winky Owens, summer residents with family ties to Provincetown, came. Tim and Mike Everett's younger brother, Toby, known affectionately as Nu Nu, was always there, never without his grape soda. The younger O'Donnell girls, Heidi and Amy, were there, as was Amy Germain. Passersby, tourists mostly, wandered in off the street, for a glimpse of the harbor — or maybe a glimpse of childhood.

If the tide was low, the kids came later and the boats sat out in the harbor, wedged in the wet flats awaiting the slightest pulse of tide to lift and float them. When we simply couldn't wait for the water to come to us, we went to it. A few of us pushed from the stern, a few more pulled from the bow, and we dragged the boats, one by one, out across the flats to the edge of the sea.

Our clubhouse was a simple structure, two-storied, blue-shuttered, with white clapboards on its face and weathered shingles on its sides. The upstairs, unfinished, was off-limits to us. We didn't question why. Many years later, during the late 1980s, when friends were running the club and using the upstairs as their summer apartment, I had my first thorough look aloft. Although the intrigue was finally satisfied, I couldn't help but feel, even then, a little bit guilty that I was where I shouldn't be.

The front door of the club was never used, rarely even opened. We used the double doors, on the side, instead. Over the front door, outside, a wrought-iron bracket held a small triangular pennant painted with the club's red, white, and blue burgee. The setback from the street was mere feet, and the stoop outside the front door became, much like Sal's wall had been, a vantage point for me to take in the world going by.

Inside was functional, a large, hollow room with two bathrooms off in a corner. Scattered four-by-fours ran floor to ceiling. The floor was plywood, strewn with boating paraphernalia, the walls unfinished, showing their studs. Just inside the double doors, the shelves were stacked with tools, boat hardware, left-behind windbreakers. Racing schedules, emergency numbers, a barometer, and a tide chart were tacked to the wall. And, too, there were the plaques to which names were added each year, plaques that reminded us of others who had gone this way, known this pleasure. To call the club rustic would be something of an overstatement. It was austere, minimal, empty of appointments but crowded with spirit. The children were its soul. The Everetts and Curbys, the Downeys and Gilmans, the Merrills and Dahills had bequeathed the club to us, the next generation. They would be forever a part of the place, their names affixed to the sailing awards that hung on the wall, securing immortality, at least within our cadre.

On any given day, life at the club unfolded much as it had the day before. We would play Chinese jump rope, hangman, cat's cradle. We'd compare yo-yo skills, play

Wiffle ball on the beach, make gum-wrapper necklaces. Straddling a beached dory, we'd set up our casino and deal the cards for blackjack. We'd climb the jetty to dive off an end rock, the one with thick algae-draped eyebrows, a head emerging from the water.

And we would play King of the Raft, turning a ten-foot-by-ten-foot square of wood and Styrofoam into a floating fortress. The best raft contests occurred when Tommy was King. A dozen of us would be in the water, desperately trying to climb aboard, almost there, only to be effortlessly picked up and tossed back by Tommy. We'd encircle the raft and plot our strategy. One of us would clutch Tommy's ankle. Another would make it up onto the raft, distracting him, while another approached from behind. We could taste victory. But it was never meant to be. It was one against an army, and the army was always vanquished. We'd finally capitulate, exhausted, wrinkled, bumped and bruised, our sinuses choked with salt water. Tommy would swim to shore where some small crisis like a broken rudder awaited his attention.

The simplicity of those days, their lack of structure and lack of worry, stay with me all these years later. I awoke in the morning, pulled on a bathing suit (if I hadn't slept in it) and an oversized T-shirt (if I hadn't slept in it), and that was it for the day. No shoes, no accessories. No messing with hair or, God forbid, any kind of face paint. The few coins I carried with me to the club I — and everyone else — set on top of the soda machine, to be retrieved when needed. No need to worry that they'd go missing. They'd be there when you got thirsty.

While others preferred the exhilarations of sailing the harbor every chance they could get, I sailed an hour or two a day, preferring to stay close to shore — a busybody, I must admit — perched out front on the stoop of the

club, curiously eyeing all that went on in the neighborhood, gabbing with folks who dropped by the club, passing a few moments with someone riding by on a bike,
helping out-of-towners. "What is the best restaurant?"
they'd asked. "Where's the beach?" "Are there sharks in
the water?" The most frequently asked question was,
"How do we get out there?" as they gestured toward Long
Point. Their eagerness turned to disappointment when I
explained that the only means were by foot along the
breakwater, in one of Flyer's boats, or with a four-wheel-
drive vehicle outfitted with all the regulation "oversand"
equipment.

The most unusual question — and not as infrequently
asked as you might imagine — concerned the monument.
"What do they do with the monument during the winter?"
the curious visitor would ask. Several among our corps
could not resist telling the innocents that just after Labor
Day the monument was lowered into the hill that it stood
on. "The weather gets mighty fierce down here in the winter, blowing in off the water as it does. A structure that
tall might not survive the storms we get down here,
storms like nowhere else because of our situation out at
sea. We just can't take the chance of losing that monument. You know, two United States presidents came
here while it was being built." And the gullible visitor
would nod his or her head as though completely understanding.

I passed hours on that stoop, beginning the day there,
whiling away a part of the afternoon, lingering on into twilight, convinced that it was the center of the universe (just
as Sal's had been when I was sitting on the wall out front).

⑥ From my perch in front of the West End Racing Club, I
would often glimpse a tiny figure, that of my grandmother,

rounding the corner of West Vine Street on her way to Perry's Market for groceries. Although we lived just around the corner from my grandmother, I saw rather little of her. Several grand mal seizures, suffered in the 1950s, had left her reluctant to go out. By the time I was older, medication had given her the confidence to go out on small errands, but she preferred to stay home, usually alone. Whenever I'd see her on her way to Perry's, I'd call out "Gramma" and cross the street to intercept her. She was always gentle, but distant. Her vocabulary was spattered with words like "dear" and "cunning," the latter a favorite of hers but now obsolete as she used it. We'd talk for a few minutes and then she'd be on her way, usually parting with an invitation to stop by the house sometime. The few times that I'd knock on her door on my way back from the Dairy Queen or a bike ride, she'd crack it open slightly and say curtly, "Not now, dear," and close the door. I had no idea what I was interrupting, perhaps her visits with her memories, but after being turned away a handful of times, I never made another attempt on my own.

I did, though, love her house, loved to explore it, and if I saw my father heading that way for a visit, I'd tag along, knowing that I could slip out undetected if I wanted to. The house, tucked away behind a dense, tall privet hedge interrupted by a flimsy, rusted gate, delighted me with its many small rooms, each of which could be closed off by a latched door. The house, with its bouncy, wide pine floors, had the wonderful smell of time, of many Cape Cod lives.

I was most intrigued by one room, the one that my grandfather had used as his studio, although nothing of his remained. When he died, leaving my grandmother with IOUs around town and little financial security, she, in her vulnerability, sold off for a pittance the contents of the studio — even his rejected, unsigned, paint-spattered watercolors, many of which still show up at auctions.

A handsome portrait of him, painted by his friend Richard Miller, hung in the living room, one of dozens of works of art that filled the house. At the far side of the living room, across from the front entrance, was my grandmother's piano. She was an accomplished pianist but had put aside her pleasures, as women of her era so often did, to tend to her family. A window with glass shelves displayed her cranberry Sandwich glass collection. Sunlight poured in through the glass, throwing blood-red slashes across the keys and throughout the room.

I remember an antique cast-iron Uncle Sam bank on a shelf in the kitchen that took my pennies when I pushed a button on its base. The bathroom, with its deep, clawfoot Victorian tub, always smelled of the tiny perfumed seashell, fish, and flower soaps that sat in a small bowl. I never knew if they were meant to be used. I felt the same about her crisp, monogrammed hand towels that were folded perfectly and draped precisely over the rail.

While my father and grandmother talked in the kitchen — and I never had any indication that the talks were anything but chatty and pleasant — the door propped open to let in the sunlight from the tiny parcel of overgrown backyard, I nosed around, lifting the latches on closed doors and opening some just enough to push my head in for a look around. I was more inquisitive than I should have been, pulling open drawers, peeking into armoires and her secretary, attracted to the leather-bound, gold-engraved book bindings, my grandfather's vibrant watercolors, the bibelots and paper silhouettes, and the old family photographs that filled every bit of wall space and every nook and cranny. There was an old steamer trunk tucked in an alcove that I desperately wanted to peek into, but it was always piled high with linens.

Behind one bedroom door, I found the carved cane my grandfather had used all his adult life, since a childhood bout with polio had weakened and withered his leg. Because virtually nothing was ever said about him — and I didn't dare ask about him because I thought it would upset my father or grandmother to remember him — his cane and his portrait held a certain mystique for me. I filled his absence with a fantasy, imagining that he would have liked me because I was his namesake's child and that I would have liked him. Had he been alive, I would have visited him and watched him paint in his studio. He might have shown me how to paint.

The narrow staircase to the upstairs was covered with a hooked runner of Cape Cod scenes that my grandmother had made and that quieted, somewhat, the creak of the steps as I went up. At the top of the stairs, a tiny closet held a trove of personal memories, carefully stacked on shelves, packets of letters, love letters I presumed, in stiff white envelopes devotedly tied with red satin ribbon. There were boxes and other papers, none of which I dared touch. Despite the excruciating temptation, I knew I was where I shouldn't be and I carefully snapped the small door closed before I was discovered. Behind another latched door, a tiny bedroom with a steeply sloping ceiling always smelled of mothballs, smelled as though whatever life had once visited had been packed away forever. I still smell that smell occasionally from someone's sweater just unpacked for a long winter, and it takes me back to that empty, sparse room, with its unadorned whitewashed walls, tiny white-painted vanity, and crisp white linens, a slant of white light squeezing through the crack in the door.

"I guess I'll be going," I'd hear my father say after an hour or so in the kitchen during those summertime visits. My curiosity satisfied (until the next visit), I'd wait out in the yard for him. He never asked what I had been doing. We'd let ourselves out the gate, stroll down West Vine, and turn the corner onto Commercial Street. I'd break off at the club.

❧ Back on my perch, I would wait for a glimpse of someone I had a schoolgirl crush on, someone from the expanding circle of friends and acquaintances, someone a few years older than I, who, though gracious in acknowledging me, didn't have a clue that my heart was racing, my stomach flip-flopping. And God forbid that he ever find out. I was delighted when he finally appeared, but relieved when he kept on walking.

I'm not sure I would have known what to do, what to say, had he stopped. While I had lots of male friends — I was always a guy's girl, the classic tomboy privy to locker-room gossip, the one they confided in when they liked a girl — boyfriends, as in the "going steady" sense, were pretty much nonexistent. My mother discouraged the boys by dressing me (she told me years later) in the most unflattering, unseductive clothes and making sure I wore my glasses. I never rebelled, never even caught on to her design, rarely considered my appearance something that I should spend any time thinking about. Not until my senior year in high school did someone express an interest in me and I wished that it had been his best friend who had asked me out.

◕ No doubt I was minding everyone else's business one afternoon when my youngest brother wandered over to the club with a kid he had met downtown. I felt an immediate connection. Extremely overweight, this kid seemed about my age and was about six feet tall with swarthy good looks; deep, clear brown eyes, kind eyes, shoulder-length hair; and a perfect, guileless smile. There was something different about him, different from everyone back home. Over the next few weeks, the last weeks of my eighteenth summer, I'd see him downtown hanging out with friends or riding around the west end on his motorcycle. He couldn't be missed in his fluorescent orange helmet.

Our friendship grew enough in those weeks that over the winter he wrote me several letters, in a childish script, telling me, with great enthusiasm, about duck hunting, his uncle's dogs, and his best friend Dickie. I always wrote back, asking about Provincetown. What he never mentioned in his letters was that all winter he had been on a diet and by spring had lost more than 100 pounds. Back in Provincetown the next May, I walked right past him downtown, shoulder to shoulder, and would have kept walking had he not called out my name. I turned around, and even then I didn't recognize him. After that day, Crayne and I were inseparable for the rest of the summer.

We would ride our bikes all over town, to the Dairy Queen, which was famous for their Dilly bars, Buster bars, and banana splits. However, we went for a cup of their kale soup. Crayne used to say, as though it was a source of pride, that Provincetown's Dairy Queen was probably the only Dairy Queen franchise in America that served kale soup. This "daily special" was something of a local secret, and the fact that I knew about it made me feel even more that I was part of the place. Every morning, one of the Portuguese women who worked at the DQ brought a bucket of the soup, thick with kale and beans and potatoes and linguica, and set it on the back burner to simmer all day, or at least as long as the soup lasted. On cool, rainy days it went fast, but on most days we could still get ourselves a cup well into evening. And the longer the soup had simmered, the better it tasted.

We would ride out to New Beach, where we'd tuck into the shadows of the jetty and talk and talk at seaside, losing all sense of time, then pedal back to the Dairy Queen to check the clock inside on the wall, hoping that it wasn't too much past the time I was expected home. A few more minutes. We would relish them as a condemned man might a reprieve. I envied him that no one seemed to be waiting for him, that he could have stayed out all night.

We'd pedal to his house, where we'd swap the bikes for his Harley or his yellow Corvette. He had only a permit to drive the Corvette and could drive it only if he was with someone who had a license. I teased him that he was only after my license because without me, the 'Vette sat in the driveway. We would drive to abandoned places — the water tower atop a dune in the east end, beach parking lots as far away as Eastham, the moors at Pilgrim Heights, the fire roads. Each night was a new adventure. With the sunroof off we'd sit for hours talking, staring up into the blackness, connecting the dots. Lying on the hood of the car, we would wish upon Perseid meteors, streaking by the dozens, lacerating an ambrosial August night. We would listen to the radio, those songs of our teen years associating themselves forever with certain moments.

He was, if nothing else, fun to be with. But he was something else. He laughed easily, a sincere laugh, and he made me laugh. We danced. We swam. We fished. He was seventeen and I was nineteen, but he made me feel nine, made me feel the simplicity, the abandon, the unencumbered happiness I had known at nine. He made me feel pretty. I had never thought I was and no one had ever told me I was, but I must have been if someone so beautiful said I was. I felt safe with him.

We would roam around downtown with the throngs, stroll down the wharf, maybe catch up with friends, Kenny or Larry. It was a friendship that I couldn't imagine would ever end, but I never considered where it needed to go next. I was in Provincetown, the place where I felt truly alive, and for me he was Provincetown. I didn't want to think beyond that.

On Labor Day weekend of that summer, we said a long good-bye out at Race Point and again behind the club. I went back to college and he sent me T-shirts, pictures of our old haunts and shoeboxes filled with whoopie pies from the Portuguese bakery. I sent him little booklets pasted with words and phrases, song titles and place names that had meaning only to us. Later in the fall he came to visit me at school, a reunion that proved awkward. He wanted more than I was capable of giving. I loved him, but I could never be in love with him. My parents would never have allowed it.

My mother had made that clear one summer afternoon when she had ordered me into the car and driven to Race Point, where she could say what she needed to say, the way she wanted to say it, without being overheard by the nosy neighbors. My father, she told me, would be furious when he got to town and learned that I was spending so much time with Crayne. I should not, she said, interpret their basic kindness toward Crayne as acceptance. Although as a boy my father had palled around with Crayne's uncles, when it came to my future, a Whorf-Provincetown Portuguese union was unacceptable. I was told in no uncertain terms that I was forbidden to get further involved. My father had always been better than that. So, in her opinion, had my mother.

I did what my mother told me to do and broke it off with Crayne, with no explanation. I knew that I had hurt him deeply, this friend who had made me feel so alive and who had brought out the best in me. After the following summer, a summer filled with bitterness, we rekindled a precarious friendship. When he moved to California, I saw him off at the airport and he would occasionally surprise me that winter with late-night calls when he had forgotten the time difference. The next summer, my last summer in Provincetown, he was back in town and I'd see him here and there, working for the family business delivering ice to restaurants, including the one where I worked. The friendship, I knew, was dying.

I thought about Crayne often, for years. I reread his cards and letters, stared at the snapshots that captured that perfect nineteenth summer. There was the night we did battle with the June bug the size of a small bird that had found its way into the car. We had pulled over onto the shoulder of Route 6, frantically batting at the bug, hoping it would find its way out the window or the sunroof. In the end it was we who were expelled from the car, tumbling in a fit of laughter into the sand where we waited until the bug flew out into the night. I don't think that I have ever laughed that hard since.

There were the handfuls of flowers he brought me, pilfered from neighborhood gardens. Baby Watson cheesecake. Flippers. James Bond movies. Ice cream cones — always chocolate chip for me — at Big Bad Wolf. Picnics at New Beach. Frisbee at a darkened Helmar's parking lot played in the warm glow of the headlights, disco pumping from the car speakers. I remember one night when we went bluefishing. We drifted in a little boat out in the hushed harbor and shared a lingering, fiery sunset, watching the tumescent orb drop like a coin into its slot behind the salt marsh. I snapped a picture with my Instamatic. We didn't get so much as a nibble, but it hardly mattered.

For years, I never forgot any of it and could never find a pretext to throw the pictures or the letters away. I did find, always, waves of dull pain, past moments revived. A song would play on the radio and I knew it instantly, within the first few notes, notes that filled me with the past. From him I could win back time.

Whenever we bumped into each other in Provincetown in the ensuing years — and it was hard not to in a town so small — the few words we managed to exchange were matter of fact, self-conscious. They could never be anything else. I could not retrieve the complete sense of invincibility that I had had with him any more than I could retrieve what I had had at Sal's. And he could not forgive me. It took me years to understand that I had clung to memories of Crayne for so long after our parting as a way of remembering who I had been, as a way of returning to a time I wanted to remember, to that seemingly perfect afternoon on the stoop at the West End Racing Club when I first set eyes on him.

֎ Out in the harbor, boats were coming and going, and if someone was looking for a not-very-serious sailing companion, I was it. If there was any one tenet from our club code of ethics to which I wholeheartedly subscribed, it was number eight — to compete for fun. I rarely raced and never won anything except an honorary burgee pin and patch for cleaning and raking the beach. I can't imagine, though, that anyone had as much fun in a sailboat as I did.

I sailed in two classes of boats — Sunfish and Robin. The appeal of the Sunfish was its ability to capsize and be righted quite effortlessly. These were bathing suits–only outings. We would get wet and go overboard. And if there happened to be a good, sustained breeze with waves slopping up and over the bow, with water bubbling around the rudder, all the better. We'd haul in the sheet and force the bullet-shaped vessel up on its side, keeping it there by lying out backward over the high side. The boat — and we, too — would scream across the harbor. We'd give another yank on the sheet and we were over, poured into the nylon sail, a triangle of stripes and color that ballooned on the water's surface. We'd float on it as on a waterbed, the hot sun beating down on us. Then we'd push against the centerboard with our feet and pull down on the hull. The Sunfish would pop upright and we'd slide aboard. Straightening the rudder, gathering in the sheet, and finding the wind, we'd pick up speed and sprint frenetically around the harbor, scavenging breeze, readying ourselves for the next dunking.

Robins were not supposed to capsize, although most of us had a mishap or two each summer. Mine happened while it was on its mooring; the boat sank like a rock and had to be towed to shore and bailed. Tommy was never amused. We didn't get wet sailing a Robin — at least we weren't supposed to — so we'd take T-shirts to protect against the sun and snacks to enjoy as we plied the harbor. Our sails were leisurely. I'd loll, draping my arm over the side, fingers skimming the water. As we'd tack back and forth, the rudder slicing through the water, the sun would be in front of one of us, then another, and another. By turns, we'd push our faces up, red sunspots behind closed eyes. I could feel the dark curtain come over my lids as we'd come about and the sail would eclipse the sun.

We'd chat, about people, of course. We would acknowledge folks passing in boats. We would watch gulls overhead stalking us, assuming we had a snack for them. When we would toss a cookie, they'd flock over and around us. The brazen ones would take the treat right from our hands. Back and forth we'd go. "Ready about," our skipper would call. "Hard alee." And she'd give the tiller a little push with her foot while we ducked to avoid the boom. I'd watch the shore, the tiny figures moving about at the club, wondering if I was missing something and hoping we didn't get becalmed. I might see Dick Santos showing the kids how to mend nets. Or Flyer, one of the club's founders, might have stopped by the club, as he did two or three times every day.

Flyer was a teacher, happy to show anyone who was hanging around how to splice or whip rope or tie knots, proper knots — bowlines, bends, and hitches. He had a style that could have been mistaken for impatience, but there were few folks in town who were as generous as Flyer was (still is) to the kids. I always loved his banter, a nonstop stream of gab that could diverge and digress only to return to the point eventually. There was little that he said that didn't offer some kind of lesson.

Every time he saw me, he told me again about the day he had moved his west-end boatyard, then just across the street from my grandparents' house at 52 Commercial Street, to the other side of the cold-storage wharf. My grandfather had often made use of the subject matter just outside his window and beyond his front door, painting pictures of the boatyard's draggers hauled up on the rail, hot with sunlight, looming in fog, subdued by twilight, or shivering in snowdrifts. "Yaw grandfatha, he cried like a baby the day I moved," remembered Flyer, who seemed flattered to have been able to provide some small dose of artistic inspiration. Flyer also had his fun with tourists who rightly took him, in his yachting cap, deep tan, khakis, and crisp T-shirt, for someone familiar with the lay of the land. "How much farther to the Red Inn?" asked out-of-towners anxious not to be late for dinner reservations. "About seven minutes up the road on your left if you walk medium," was Flyer's straight-faced reply. The recipient, you could tell, didn't know what to make of it. Or him.

We would gather around Flyer for knot-tying lessons: first we learned the names — standing part, bight, end, turn — then watched intently as Flyer snapped the line over into a loop, fed the free end through the loop, under the standing end, and back through the loop. All the while he would chatter on and seemingly pay no attention to the rope itself. He'd pull it tight. We'd all then have a go of it, tangling ourselves in the line, barely able to get out of our own way. But after some practice most of us got the hang of it, got pretty good at tossing clove hitches over the pilings and tying our sections of rope into bowlines and squares. I wish I could say I never again used an improper knot. But I confess I did. Still do. Somehow, when that small length of rope that we'd practiced on became a long length of rope with a boat or anchor attached to one end, it just seemed easier to tie four or five stopper knots and hope and pray that they would hold.

When we sailors would finally return to shore, feel the hull slide into the sand as the centerboard was hauled up and secured, I would be relieved to be able to resume my favorite pastime: hanging around. I'd gather in the sail, unclip the rudder, climb the short, planked staircase whose steps had been worn and rounded by so many others before me, and stomp the sand from my feet.

⚓ "Make yourself useful," I think Tommy said one afternoon when I was doing my usual nothing and the beach was particularly congested with seaweed carried in by an offshore storm. He handed me a rake. From then on, my beach cleanups became regular happenings.

I employed the methods that I had perfected at Sal's, scanning the beach, eyes darting left to right, ever ready to make a discovery. First I'd tackle the thick windrow of tumbled eel grass, blackened rockweed, and Spartina

tubes that had entrapped pearly jingle shells, mermaids'
purses, transparent horseshoe crab sheds, pebbles, crab
claws, and curls of sea lettuce. As soon as I had disturbed
a pile, there came an onslaught of lively beach hoppers. As
the tide receded, I would confront the intertidal space.

Here was a different kind of trove and I, no longer a
mere beachcomber, was an archeologist. It was a landfill,
really, and buried in it were the remnants of an earlier
time when working wharves issued from the shore and
folks thought nothing of tossing their trash into the sea,
expecting that the outgoing tide would carry it all away.
Glass, tin cans, hardware, paint cans, engine parts, liquor
bottles, sheet metal, chunks of concrete, tires, and broken
tools all went overboard into the harbor and, eventually,
into the sand, at least partly. Wooden troughs brought
raw toilet sewage dribbling down the beach from homes.

Besides raking a variety of seaweeds, I unearthed enormous shipworm-chewed logs, probably sections of old pilings, and planks with heavy, rusted spikes. Disturbing
these subterranean dwellers added to my work — there
being so much more buried than visible — but having
started, I dug and pulled and dug and pulled some more
until finally they were dislodged with a loud sucking
sound as the wet sands caved in.

I found old coins, eroded by the salt water except for one
tiny spot that identified it as a dime or nickel rather than a
washer. Glass and pottery shards were everywhere. Pieces
that had been tossed and tumbled by the sea were rounded
and frosted; pieces that had been buried in the sand, still
sharp and clear. I saved the frosted glass — bits of medicine
and liquor bottles — that came in fire reds, cobalt blues,
mellow yellows, and spring greens, as well as bits of pottery
with interesting design fragments, and slipped them into
my bathing suit as I had once done with shells.

It was not just debris I was uncovering, but time capsules, buried when wharves had extended a thousand feet out to sea. Back then, two- and three-masted vessels had crowded the harbor like the stately beeches out in the dune forest. Dory sails had been hoisted, drying in the sun. Laundry, too. The packet from Boston had rounded Long Point, depositing passengers downtown, who mingled with passengers just off the train. Horse-drawn jiggers had carried away luggage. Clothiers, billiard halls, fish merchants, meat markets, striped barber poles, and mortars and pestles had been sprinkled around the downtown. Coal, wood, Moxie, cigars, and tobacco had been advertised in painted, bold Helvetica letters on rooftops and on the sides of buildings. On the beach, fishermen had been busy knitting nets, scraping hulls, and repairing gear. Others had sat on fish boxes in front of their sheds on the beach, whittling, playing whist or the Jew's harp, and chewing on the dried, rock-hard fish they called Skully Joe. Their voices had rung out in broken English or Portuguese. And that immortal stench of fish hung in the air.

My cleanup finished, I would look over the beachscape with a sense of accomplishment, the pile of flotsam and jetsam on the beach evidence of my work. I knew only too well that within days, the sea and sand would disgorge more castoffs.

෨ Like Sal's, the club was quiet on rainy days. The double doors would be propped open, but the kids didn't come, choosing to stay home rather than just hang out. I, of course, preferred to just hang out, and so I would go.

From the bench behind the club, I remember watching the flannel-soft fog roll in, creating a seamless sea and sky, creeping and seeping, planting its damp kisses in every corner and crevice, its arrival announced by the lament of the foghorn out beyond Long Point. In front of me, rain fell, pocking the sand, bubbling the harbor. The stairs and deck overhead kept me dry except for a steady drip that had found its way through the planking. Slowly, the fog obliterated Long Point across the harbor, the green vegetated dune tops and the yellow beach. Sometimes the fog would spread across the harbor and in front of the Point in a narrow, low-lying band, seeming to lop off and levitate the tops of the hills. Sometimes, if the fog wasn't dense but instead a transparent veil of blue, it gave a wavy, watery appearance to Long Point, making it seem more an apparition than a real place.

A wind shift sent the boats spinning on their moorings. The water was purple and green, sometimes black. The ha ha ha of gulls echoed in the quiet that settled in with the fog. An outboard engine purred somewhere unseen. The damp hung inside the club. Whoever showed up was put to work mending sails, replacing hardware, sweeping sand, cleaning bathrooms, refilling the soda machine. If the rain had been heavy, and if the harbor wasn't too roiled, we went out in the skiff to bail the sailboats.

It was on one of these rainy, foggy days that I was given the task of dressing up the club's interior with pictures. I was appointed, I supposed, because of my painterly family and the presumption, mistaken as it turns out, that I, too, could paint. My father called such a presumption, which was — and still is — being perpetuated by certain family members who fancy themselves artists by virtue of their pedigree alone, the "myth of the artistic gene."

"I can't paint," I protested, but was nonetheless pressed into service with the encouraging words, "Anything is better than bare wood. Don't worry, if it's really bad we can paint over it." Getting started, as always, was the hardest part. I was given complete freedom to choose my design,

and I decided that the middle of the floor was the place
for a large compass rose. I looked around for something to
copy. "You don't expect me to do this by memory," I
protested, and found a tiny compass rose at the top of a
tide chart. On one of the walls I sketched out an outline of
Cape Cod with a big star at the tip to designate Provincetown. Inside one of the bathroom doors I planned my version of the monument, and on the outside of the doors,
the labels Gulls and Buoys, which didn't seem at all corny
at the time. Across the rafters I spelled out "West End
Racing Club" in international flags. Over the next few
days I labored happily to the Top Forty with my paints,
the bright greens and reds, yellows and blues, and a con-
coction of them all as close to gray as I could get for the
monument. The plywood floors drank up my colors,
requiring many coats of paint and several coats of poly-
urethane to seal the mural's fate. I was actually quite satisfied with the results. My name, I knew, would never
appear on the plaques for marlinspike seamanship or for
sailor of the year, but I had left my own mark, hoping my
masterpieces might survive the summer, perhaps longer.

Stepping Out

MY TIME AT THE CLUB began to be abbreviated when I landed my first real job (something other than a paper route) when I was seventeen. Nearing the end of high school and with college in my plans, I was expected to contribute a little something toward my education. My father arranged for me to run errands and do light housework for an older woman, Mrs. Constance Carpenter, who had been a close friend of my grandparents. She lived in the far west end, way up along, as they used to say, in a lovely home on the beach, which was hidden from passersby on Commercial Street by a dense, tall privet hedge.

Mr. Carpenter had passed on a few years earlier, and Mrs. Carpenter was living alone in the house. I still have the letter she wrote, in an unsteady but determined hand. "Yes. I am very sure that I would like to have you work, not for but with me this summer. . . . I would like to have you help me for about four hours each day except Sunday, probably from 8:30 to 12:30. I would pay by the hour — $2.50 an hour. . . . I have a car — automatic shift."

One morning each week, before beginning any chores, I was dispatched to the donut shop out on Shankpainter Road to fetch a dozen donuts. I remember this vividly, not only because it was part of the routine but because these donuts, jelly donuts, square-shaped, were the most delicious things I'd ever tasted. With my own money, I would buy two or three to eat on my bike ride back to the west end, careful to wipe any jelly or sugar off my mouth so that Mrs. Carpenter would not suspect. She would not have cared, I'm sure, but I didn't want to do anything to jeopardize the snack that awaited me later in the morning. I couldn't risk having her say, "Oh, I see you've already had your donuts this morning, then you won't be wanting another!" I couldn't take that chance and so was meticulous about hiding the evidence, wiping every last sugar granule and speck of jelly off my face. As the morning wore on, all I could think about were those donuts, on her counter in a brown bakery box, waiting to be popped into the toaster oven, to be cooked so that the outside was crisp, the inside soft, the jelly warm. The moment would finally come, midmorning. She never forgot. She would invite me to sit in her kitchen, and she would share not only donuts — one each so that they would last the entire week — and milk, but also her memories of my grandparents. She was kind, gentle, somewhat frail, but tough in an old Cape Cod sort of way. I never asked about her family, if she had any children, never thought it was my place. I had no idea how old she was. I did, however, ask about the handsome bronze bells that were hanging in her yard, lashed with chains to frames made of old ships' timbers.

They were Spanish bells that she and her late husband, Ralph, had brought back from Cuba, where he had managed a sugar plantation back in the teens after their marriage. After leaving Cuba, they had come to Provincetown and built the Delft Haven cottages, a tidy compound of rental cottages on the beach next to their home. The bells that had once hung in Spanish missions were now ornaments in Mrs. Carpenter's garden, hanging in front of her seawall, mixed in with Rosa rugosa, pines, and perennials. Though Mrs. Carpenter's house was not unusual, like the Murchison's Bauhaus house, that grand house across the street, there was for me an old-world aristocratic feel about it that set it off from other spots in town. Sal's Place had a Mediterranean charm, but in a humbler, everyman's sense. Mrs. Carpenter's home, with its brick-and-stone patio, gleaming white facade, and Spanish bells, could have been a villa tucked away on a hillside in Havana. Maybe the Carpenters, like Sal, had been trying to create something there in the west end that reminded them of a happy time from their past.

From the living room, a large plate-glass window gave an unobstructed sea and sky panorama across the harbor to Long Point. Perpendicular to the window, on the wall over a sofa, hung a magnificent seascape by Frederick Waugh, who, better than any other marine painter, articulated the dynamic and structure of water. The painting had been given to the Carpenters in a trade that Waugh had made for a mission bell that he, in turn, gave to St. Mary's of the Harbor, which he founded. A pair of Spanish pistols rested barrel-crossed on a living room shelf. Works of art were scattered throughout the house, including, in a small back room, three watercolors by my grandfather of a luscious nude in the dunes. The flesh tones were so real, so translucent, that I half expected this young lady to turn around, right there in the frame, and tell me to stop staring at her derriere. In a downstairs bathroom there was a small abstract work by Karl Knaths, a modernist whose studio was across the street from the Carpenters. The placement of the picture — a squiggly, colorful thing, as I remember it — there in the water closet always struck me as odd. I wondered if Mr. Knaths was insulted that his creation was relegated to the room where one's more private business took place. Or was he flattered that it was placed where it could be admired in peace and solitude?

The morning's chores included vacuuming, during which I had to be instructed, repeatedly, to slow down in order to pick up from deep within a rug's pile. When Mrs. Carpenter demonstrated, I felt a calm come over me as she gently pushed the humming machine. Down in the laundry room, that same sense of calm, a kind of tingly, relaxed feeling when you tune out of the moment and travel to some far-off place, overcame me as we folded sheets. She always took them from the dryer slightly damp. We would lie them out on long tables and fold them in half lengthwise, then in half again, then my end to hers, and again, and on each fold she would show me how to hand-iron, pressing out the wrinkles with soothing, short strokes of her wrinkled hands. It was a kind of mantra and I would often go off into a trance watching her, hoping that it would not end, the smooth rhythm, the calm, the dignity that could be contained in so ordinary an act.

⑥ I worked for Mrs. Carpenter only that one summer. The next two summers I washed dishes and made salads and sandwiches at the Cottage, a restaurant at the edge of downtown. Owned by the Feltons and managed by Dick Felton and his partner, Horace, the Cottage had a family atmosphere and attracted a gay clientele, especially on Sundays when the Bloody Marys flowed like the Congo. This was my first real immersion in the gay scene, which, in those pre-AIDS 1970s, was working its way to carefree and flamboyant levels. However, my most vivid memory of the Cottage is of the cook, Ruth, a robust middle-aged woman from town who whacked away at scrambled eggs with her wide utensil and had little patience for the proprietors' frequent emotional crises.

Out in the front lounge patrons chased away hangovers with more booze and stared at the television, watching the final act of the national Watergate drama. Closer to home, we had our own drama. A young woman was found gruesomely murdered in the dunes, her hands cut off, her skull smashed in, her face decomposing in the sand, her toenails painted pink, her hair tied in a ponytail, her dungarees neatly folded under her. I remember reading the newspaper account on my lunch break at work and feeling a terrible anxiety and fear. I often wandered in the dunes and had been out in the dunes at Race Point just the day before the body was found. Without knowing any of the details surrounding the crime, I wondered that day while reading the newspaper, Was this a random crime? Wrong place, wrong time? Could it have been me?

One of the waitresses speculated that the killer was someone the girl knew, maybe had met in a bar. I willingly embraced that notion because I could avoid a similar fate simply by never inviting a stranger into my life. I had control over that circumstance. What I didn't have control over was someone lurking in the lonely dunes waiting for an unsuspecting young solitary to wander past.

Despite its share of miscreants and vagrants, its reputation for the zany, even the kinky, Provincetown had never been a place where one feared for one's life. We didn't think anything of venturing out alone, deep into the woods or dunes or out onto an empty stretch of beach, or of walking to the farthest end of town alone at four in the morning. If a child was out of the parents' sight, they feared a drowning more than a stranger. The chilling crime, with its chilling newspaper headline — "Victim Found on Back Shore Dune" — didn't steal our freedom, but as the weeks wore on and no arrest was made and as rumors began circulating that another young woman's body had been found, not a few folks wondered if the individual who could commit such brutality on another human being was still in our midst. It gave us all pause for thought.

After twenty-seven years, the "Woman in the Dunes" mystery was again in the news. The victim's remains were exhumed from a humbly marked Provincetown grave for DNA testing. As a detective who had chased leads in the case for more than a decade, Provincetown police sergeant Warren Tobias was prepared to make an arrest in the case if DNA confirmed that the victim was the Plymouth County jail escapee police suspected she was. Disappointingly, DNA tests proved conclusively that the victim was not who police had long believed her to be. The case remains open and unsolved, and the whereabouts of the escapee is still unknown.

Despite a new awareness of danger and vulnerability, my world was expanding, the sirens downtown calling to me. Although there was still nourishment in the west end, my sustenance came more and more from downtown, from the energy that was unleashed when the crowds came. And the crowds did come — a human bouillabaisse. Seasonal workers came — busboys, waitresses, chambermaids, gift-shop clerks. Suburban couples, with baby strollers and preteens. College kids, with their bikes, bound for the narrow paved trails that snaked through the dunes. By tour bus grandmotherly types came, in white pantsuits, with white sandals, white handbags, and white hair done blue for the outing. Lost souls, aging hippies, street musicians with their guitar cases open to collect spare change, chanting, drumming Krishnas, starving artists, drag queens, same-sex lovers, ménages à trois, leather, lace — all came.

They came for the designer boutiques, honky-tonk souvenir shops, gourmet ice-cream stands, foot-long hot dogs, haute cuisine, Paris-style sidewalk cafés, pizza joints, gay discos, upscale New York–owned, avant-garde art galleries, saltwater-taffy shops, Mediterranean color, and Pilgrim history. They came for the freedom to be themselves, the permission that Provincetown gave them to take an excursion into the forbidden. They came to Provincetown thinking themselves the gawkers, when in fact everyone who stepped foot in the place became the gawked at, players in the unfolding summer drama, sometimes melodrama and not infrequently farce. Many were content just to take in the plein air pageant from the benches — the meet (meat?) racks in front of Town Hall — appalled but also titillated by things they'd never seen, would never see, back home.

The place was an original, had a proud contempt for all social convention, a distinctive character that never reflected society in general. Where else would the town drunk and the Pilgrim-garbed Town Crier gladly share the same slab of sidewalk? Where else would irreverent, ungroomed, reeking counterculture types and urbane, gray-templed, well-dressed New York Times editors be invited to the same dinner party? Where else but in Provincetown would the burial of an old junkbox car in someone's backyard inspire poetry and merit a champagne toast? Where else could a swan in auburn wig, red heels, and gold-sequined miniskirt belt out a Judy Garland tune, a cappella, in the middle of downtown and not be thought deranged? Where else could an old codger keep a live quahog as a pet? Where else would folks forsake given names for sobriquets like Grassie, Barshi, Boyzine, Ducky, Pinky, and Ding?

I was immersed deeper into the downtown scene the next summer when I worked at Café Poyant, a busy, sidewalk café smack in the middle of town. Vehicular and pedestrian traffic moved along Commercial Street without interruption, day and night, with the speed of viscous lava. At work, the pace all day was frantic: the same sandwiches, held together with fringed toothpicks, pushed out onto the shelf from the small kitchen, garnished with radishes, pickles or crackers, delivered along with frothy, overfilled drinks to the same tightly squeezed-together, checkered-clothed tables over and over and over again. It got so that I was grateful for a poetry-writing coffee drinker who occupied the table for forty-five minutes. Never mind the tips I was losing; it was one table I didn't have to worry about. After work, I joined the street crowd as I made my way home to the west end on my bike. You'd think the all-day dose of throbbing excess would have been quite enough. No. The sirens called me back. I wanted, needed, to be part of it, and I was, every night.

After dark the crowd was thicker, more convivial, boisterous, coiling around stalled traffic in the design of a double helix. Townies in their jazzed up cars, with radios blaring everything from the Rolling Stones to the Archies, cruised by, making the loop — along Commercial Street to Court Street, up to Bradford Street, and back down Bradford to Standish Street — and easing back into the flow along Commercial Street, ready for another pass, ready to see and be seen again. After a handful of laps, they broke out of the routine, detoured out to New Beach to see what was happening, to see who was there, then resumed their regular route. It went on like this all night.

Lusty disco music, with its incessant percussion and sexual hum, belched from nightclubs into Commercial Street, where it coalesced in a confusing din. The smells were no less overwhelming: salt air, seafood, steaks, fudge, warm tar, exhaust, cheap colognes, expensive colognes, perspiration, pot, incense, and lust. So swept along in this tunnel of hedonistic energy were we that we had no sense of the infinite black sky overhead nor of the vast open space just beyond.

I spent hours hanging out in front of Town Hall, at the meet racks but never on them (only tourists actually sat on the benches), taking in the parade of exhibitionists strutting their stuff on the Commercial Street catwalk. Each one upped the ante: the man in the cowboy chaps with his buttocks hanging out trying to outdo the man in the tutu with his genitals hanging out trying to outdo the man wrapped in pink cellophane with everything hanging out.

Our sidewalk circle now included my brother John and our friend Russell. Like me, Russell had family ties to Provincetown and came with his parents and sisters for the summer. They stayed at his grandmother's house on Conant Street on the edge of downtown. Russell lived a normal life the rest of the year in a blue-collar suburb of Boston and, like me, had a difficult time explaining to friends back home what he did on his summer vacation. You just had to be there.

We'd occupy the sidewalk, ready in an instant to hop onto a tailgate for the ride through town, to dash out into the street to gab with someone in a car, never minding that our little indulgence was backing up already backed-up traffic. As the evening wore on, we'd drift from the street into one nightclub or another, to the Old Colony, a fisherman's watering hole. Thanks to Russell's friendship with Eddie, the bartender, we could drink on the house, talking to sessile barfly-philosophers who had, it seemed to us, answers to all of life's questions. The talk was usually so banal that we figured it had to be profound. Someone would read us poems from a small journal held together by rubber bands. "You should have those published," we'd insist, thinking his creations brilliant. For a double shot of vodka, someone else would doodle for us on napkins and sketch our caricatures with a thick black marker on that day's newspaper. "You should show your stuff to a gallery," we'd insist, thinking his creations brilliant.

We'd tumble off the bar stools out onto Commercial Street and on to the Back Room and the A-House, gay discos with brain-bashing sound systems, revolving overhead colored lights, flashing floor lights, and patrons possessed by the music. Just try to sit still for that music. We couldn't. We'd take to the dance floor, surrounded by golden, immaculate, coiled homosexual boys. After a few songs, we'd be on our way.

We subscribed to the Byronic notion that if you stop, you think; if you think, you're sorry. We'd take in a set at the Surf Club, the strictly straight bar at the head of Town Wharf where the Jug Band, a group of local guys with names like Geno, Moe, and Joe Bones, accompanied themselves on banjo, trombone, washboard, spoons, harmonica, and washtub and played Tin Pan Alley songs of the thirties and forties. The Surf Club was a locals' place, a rough, ramshackle bar hanging out over the beach, built of old ships' timbers where dozens of hats, used in the act, hung from the rafters. It was one of my favorite places, a place I had been going to since before I was of legal age, allowed in only because I was accompanied by a group of town guys for whom the proprietor turned a blind eye. I drank Pepsi all night while they chased shots of Chartreuse with Bud. And one of them always delivered me home safely and at a reasonable hour. Several summers later, long after most of the town kids had grown weary of the Jug Band and their predictable act and bad jokes, I continued to make my pilgrimage, night after night, introducing anyone new to our group to the place.

We had no particular design; only a quenchless need to go. We added to our numbers, yoking ourselves to the crew from the Red Inn, who were making their way to the

Governor Bradford for an after-work game of foosball. I had first set eyes on Billy, Clay, Paul, and Jimmy late one afternoon at the West End Racing Club, where they were taking Tommy up on a water-skiing invitation. There was a certain élan about that group, standing there in T-shirts and gym shorts with boxer shorts hanging out a few inches below the hem, with tousled, longish, sun-lightened hair, deep tans, athletic physiques, and confidence that had been ladled out in such quantities that someone else, somewhere, probably was doing without. They were all from Vermont, relatives and friends of the Barker family who owned the Red Inn, an elegantly appointed beachfront restaurant in the west end next to Mrs. Carpenter's house. Billy and I became fast friends, and the others accepted me by virtue of that friendship.

They epitomized that bumper sticker, Whoever dies with the most toys wins. Jeeps, sailboats, speedboats, bikes, water skis — their generosity was as considerable as their possessions. What was theirs was yours. When I was not working, I was at the Red Inn, swimming, boating, barbecuing with them on the beach until it was time for them to go to work. Occasionally I would work a night washing dishes at the Red Inn, happy just to be near Billy, to share his world. On his nights off, we'd hang out in the early evening at a converted garage where most of the guys stayed all summer, draping ourselves over the bed, listening to the Eagles and Linda Ronstadt, talking big philosophies, talking about most everything except tomorrow.

Others would drift in and join the conversation, and at some point we'd all shift over to Jimmy's house, next door to the restaurant. An affectionate bear of a guy who was a little older than I, Jimmy, who is deaf, loved to roughhouse, dance, and narrate long, detailed jokes that had me doubled over, gasping for air, my sides splitting with laughter. He was Ted and Marci Barker's son, Paul's brother, and more than any of the others, Jimmy made me feel welcome at the Red Inn. His house was usually filled with friends visiting from school, their hands and fingers pouring out conversation. In many ways I think that I knew Jimmy better than I knew the others. His signals never seemed mixed and I never had to guess what he was feeling. He always looked me right in the eye and said what he meant. He told me once that he loved me and I believed him, knew exactly how he meant it.

We'd swig beer, watch reruns of Your Show of Shows on a snowy black-and-white television, play blackjack or charades, listen to music. Although I had little interaction with Mr. and Mrs. Barker or with their oldest boys, the environment that they had created was not unlike that at Sal's, a kind of fluid system that renewed the sense of safety and belonging that I had always felt at Sal's. They seemed to subscribe to the simple idea that if one of their kids liked you, they liked you. Around ten, we'd head into town.

The Governor Bradford was a shots-of-tequila hangout for grungy bikers in leather jackets who lingered in the smoke-filled room, waiting to shoot pool or play foosball. There was always a feeling that at any moment someone might pick a fight. The Bradford was never a favorite haunt of mine, and if we did stop in, it wasn't for long. We'd soon quit the downtown and eagerly make our way out to Piggies, a denlike dance bar with a straight clientele where so many of my evenings ended, where I lost myself in the elixir of disco music on a crowded dance floor. The songs the DJ played became anthems for my existence: "I Gotta Keep Dancing," "Twenty-Four Hours a Day."

The music would pulse. During the evening furtive looks were caught, touches stolen. Couples would huddle in the shadows fulfilling their desires. The music would unleash fantasies, as did the glass vials that were snapped open, passed around, and inhaled. Invitations were whispered — "Want to go somewhere after this?" By eleven, the dance floor would be filled. The pitch would heighten, all thinking stop, legs lock between legs. Bodies, unleashed by the music, would press together and undulate as one. The fast dances had carried everyone out to the edge; the DJ would pull them back with a slow song. Drenched in sweat, I'd retreat to the edge of the dance floor to catch my breath, cool my face and the back of my neck with a frosty beer bottle.

At one A.M., the lights would flicker and the exodus from the lair would begin. Outside, we'd linger in the cool, dark beginning of the new day, the parking lot dusty and churned up by departing vehicles. We'd walk back into town, still possessed by the night's energy. Hundreds of patrons from dozens of nightclubs would pour onto Commercial Street, most making their way in thick procession to Spiritus Pizza. For anyone who did not want to go home alone but had not yet made arrangements, this was the last opportunity, and the efforts were all too often desperate.

The Red Inn boys and I — Johnny, Russell, and anyone else who wanted to join us — would plunk down on the curb, devouring our slices and gulping oversized Pepsis while we took in the scene, a great peaceful mingling of people, young and old, male and female, gay and straight, tourist and townie. In Provincetown there was no past, no tomorrow, only the now, today, this minute, which is why everyone lingered there in front of Spiritus, and no one wanted to go home even though it was past 3 A.M.

Long Point

LONG POINT'S two lighthouses stand about a mile
apart on a brushstroke of sand under a dome of sky. What
anyone who visits here notices right away is the vast openness. That there can be a place like Long Point so close to a
teeming summer resort is due to its isolation and inacces-
sibility. You need a private boat or the inclination to cross,
by foot, the mile-long riprap breakwater. There are no
facilities and virtually no shade. The only refuge is in the
slanting shadows of the lighthouses.

There is also a lack of variety — a few bird types, not
much more vegetation, and a couple of sand hillocks and
dune swales to give the land some texture. And silence.
The kind of quiet that impelled me to confront my own
thoughts, or the lack of them; my self, or the absence of
any strong sense of self; my resourcefulness, or its defi-
ciency. And aloneness. Not so much being alone, but
being unoccupied in that aloneness. Few visitors to
Provincetown really explore Long Point, although many
venture across the breakwater. They investigate nearby
Wood End Light, maybe have a look at the bay side, with
its friskier waters, a few steps away. But they look along
the inside shoreline, along the curve of Long Point to its
tip, through all the space between the lights. They are
apprehensive. The struggle is too elemental, the rewards
too simple, the emptiness too threatening. The sirens
don't sing on Long Point, not the way they do across the
harbor in Provincetown.

When I was younger, Long Point with its trim white-washed lighthouses was little more than a destination that gave some purpose to my meanderings in a boat. Not that I needed a destination. For me, it was enough simply to be moving, to be busy in space. When I was boating in the harbor, within the embrace of Long Point, there was always something happening, and I never much cared if I arrived anywhere. If I did manage to end up at the Point, I'd collect a few shells, take a dip, or check to see if the coastguardsman in charge of the lighthouse had forgotten to lock up so that I could get inside — he never had — then I returned to my travels.

The West End Racing Club held its annual picnic at the Point every August to put our sailing skills to the test; tacking back and forth across the harbor, we'd eventually land our vessels just west of the jetty at Long Point Light. We'd set sail first thing in the morning, crossing the harbor in a convoy of Sunfish, Robins, and Boston Whalers with perhaps a lone rowboat pulling up the distant rear. We'd spend the day on the Point, about seventy-five of us, swimming and snorkeling; a lucky one among us might find a bed of sand dollars. We'd cooked hot dogs on a makeshift grill, toss Frisbees, belly-board behind the club skiff, and of course, work on our sailing skills.

When I was young, I paid little attention to the light-houses, thinking them nothing more than the practical, requisite ornaments of any peninsula worth its salt, never thought of them as objects of romance, as perpetuating the memory of another time, before electronic navigation, when the sea gave nothing "except hard knocks," as Joseph Conrad wrote; nor did I ever consider the lighthouse keeper — Long Point's had long been replaced by the electronic version — as a metaphor for the confrontation with self. Never did I pause to inhale the delicate fragrance of the *Rosa rugosa* that then scrambled all along the dune edge. Nor did I explore Long Point's landscape, except to wander out to the very tip, just to be able to say that I could go no farther. I clung to our group, to humanity, to the water's edge, to that view across the harbor, to that bohemia that so entranced me.

But over time, imperceptibly, my affection for Long Point grew. Once seen by me as a forlorn outpost, Long Point became a place full of events, defining moments, a place full of possibilities, where the quiet had something to say.

I began escaping to Long Point for brief respites after work, liberated from the congested and noisy downtown that I had been immersed in all day. It was a relief to temporarily escape people and my responsibility to people. For a few hours I could, in the peacefulness of Long Point, nurture an inner life, though not an inner world of flight-taking imagination or fantasy. I was not by nature one who created or retreated to fantastic places or got lost wandering in literature's make-believe, not much of a dreamer. My place had always been in the here and now. What inner life I had was the nascent stirring of reflection — sorting, questioning, doubt.

By the summer I was 19, my family had traded in the aluminum motorboat for a Boston Whaler, shining white, the summer sun glinting off the hull. Eminently seaworthy and great fun, it made the trip to Long Point an adventure, skimming across the harbor on flat, calm days, bucking like a wild stallion when the sea got choppy.

Not enough good things can be said for Provincetown harbor as a boater's companion, although it's not always a congenial companion. Like any friend, it can be disagreeable and is better left alone when in that mood. Most of the time, though, it is an accommodating friend, a magnificent natural deepwater harbor out beyond the tidal flats with deepwater access, sheltered, with little current, a gentle grade, no underwater hazards, a superb anchorage, coarse, heavy sand, and no mud. The water was so clear that I could navigate simply by watching the surface color — blue-black or green-black at its deepest points, a chain of blond sandbars changing the color to the turquoise of a Caribbean lagoon in the shallows. At the Point, summer's pace was always as it should be — lazy, languid, like a fishing line paying out astern on a trolling boat.

At its westernmost end, behind the breakwater, the salt marsh teemed with life. On the last moments of the high tide, water poured into the salt marsh from the harbor through the polygons of rock, crashing, raging, cascading out the other side where its fury was broken by the meadow. The tide unfurled, flowing into tidal creeks, a warm blush through a body, depositing sediment, nourishing every extremity and appendage.

At high tide, a depression in the trapezoidal stack of granite would afford just enough width and depth necessary for my boat, outboard lifted, to float over the ligature on a pulse of current and into the marsh. I would drift noiselessly in this Barbizon landscape of plush greens, *Spartina* grasses, waving, parting like a receiving line as my snub bow nosed through. I was intimate with this otherwise inaccessible field as no beach walker could ever be, a participant rather than a spectator. Beyond the vast flatness of the marsh, whose grasses were mowed naturally by winter's ice, the spine of Long Point wrapped around and flowed into the sands of the Great Beach. Beyond Long Point lay the open bay into which life plunged after leaving this womb.

Here was a world fragile, delicate, a prairie of apple green, dusty green, pickle green, embellished later in the summer with the dainty purple of sea lavender. Quivering waters, glowing light, warm, moist, whispering wind masked the commotion beneath. The salt marsh was diverse, fecund, sensual; the grasses anchored and knotted life. Each element, despite the apparent randomness and independence, worked in synchrony, one taking nourishment from another.

The shadows of the rippling, running surface marbleized the spongy salt marsh peat. Underneath, a vast network of grass roots sprawled, sending out runners that appeared as stubby shoots in spring, growing and advancing the marsh. Shellfish, worms, fiddler crabs, and sand eels were secreted away. There was flirting and mating as the marsh filled with blooms of egg and sperm. Minnows schooled; air pockets bubbled; periwinkles and coffee bean snails grazed; scallops and pipefish played hide-and-seek in the eel grass; hinged shells, spread open like butterfly wings, littered the floor; crispy, fat, firm glasswort soaked up salt water. Rimming the marsh was a collar of beach pea, goldenrod, sea rocket, thistle, blueberry, bearberry, bayberry, Virginia creeper, Virginia rose, groundsel, and poison ivy, each with its own season. The whole place was tinged with a malodor, the smell of decay necessary for life. The salt marsh was a microcosm of that one great process described by Thoreau as the passing away of one life to make way for another. I would drift in this holy place, stretched out in the bow of my boat, under the sweet glaze of the sun. Overhead, a bird would caw and somewhere far off the tide would still bubble through the rocks. Nearby, the grasses would sigh with softness.

I had too little time to indulge. The flowing tide would finish. At slack water, all the world stood still. Then, with an about-face, the tide would march once again and I'd catch a pulse that would drift me up and over the breakwater and back out into the harbor. The water would withdraw

through the rocks, crashing, raging, cascading, and draining the marsh.

Hugging the shoreline, I'd make my way past Lobster
Plain, past the twin hills, to the jetty near the tip of Long
Point, the spot of earlier club picnics. There was satisfac-
tion in not being able to go any farther.

⑤ And there at that tip, atop a small but sturdy dune liberal with *Rosa rugosa*, was a wooden cross. It had always
been there, directly across the harbor from A Home at
Last, weathering gales, blistering heat, numbing cold. I
had assumed that it was a fisherman's memorial until one
day, on Sal's patio — I was eleven or twelve — someone
mentioned the cross. Sal, a member of that male fellowship of artists who called themselves Beachcombers, of
which my grandfather had proudly held the office of Skipper, explained that the cross was a memorial to fellow
Beachcomber Charles Darby, a young man who had discovered Provincetown and fallen under its spell in the early
thirties. He had been killed in action in 1944.

More than twenty-five years after hearing Sal talk about
the cross, I was reading microfilm at the Art Archives in
Boston for a graduate-school project about Provincetown's
art colony when I happened upon the Beachcombers'
papers and scrapbooks. Included with the minutes of their
Saturday night confabs, I found an uninhibited letter, written from England and dated September 14, 1944, from
Charles Darby to my grandfather. The two had been close
friends for a decade, Darby a few years younger than my
grandfather. In the last part of his letter Darby remembered Provincetown:

*I've been busy working most of the time. I still think of
Provincetown and coming back there some day but god knows*

when I will. It can't last much longer over here but I don't have
a hope of coming back when this one is over — and I hate like
hell to think of two more such years somewhere else. So help
me if I ever get out of this I'll never set foot in a god damn
bloody airplane again.

I read in the Advocate *about the 'Combers having a Ball —*
but never heard how it was. Good I hope. By god, John, you
don't know what I'd give to be back there sometimes — fall
afternoon, chili cooking on the stove and fine new bottle of
whiskey standing by — perhaps a pale ray of late sun shining
through it. A week ago we collected some fine souvinir [sic] *and*
drank it every bit up — first time I ever drank champagne out
of a canteen cup — everybody got fine and tight and it did
remind me of those days at the club. It took a magnum to cheer
me up when I thought about it. I shore [sic] *did cheer up good*
though. Best of everything to you John and all — CHARLES

I advanced the microfilm. The next frame contained the
Western Union telegram dated November 5, 1944, from
Charles's father to my grandfather:

MY SON DIED ON THE 17TH SOMEWHERE OVER HOLLAND

After a brief, handwritten note of condolence from my
grandfather, Mr. Darby replied:

Charles loved me dearly as he did his mother, but in spite of
this we were never able to keep him with us more than a month
at Christmas. After discovering Provincetown and making
friends there the pull was too strong — he just could not resist
it, the place had the greatest fascination for him, but his
friends exercised the greatest pull and he loved the quaintness
of the place, the bright sunlight & ocean, & sweeps of the lonely
sand downs with the wild sand roses of which he talked to me

incessantly, but it was the friends of which he never tired of
telling me about.

And then a father's pained request, that a plaque might be fastened to a stone and set, overlooking the ocean, in the lonesome sand dunes, a memorial to an unsung soldier.

At the next meeting of the Beachcombers there was a motion "that a cross be made for Darby. The motion was seconded by Whorf and carried." Dedicated on the lawn of the Provincetown Art Association, the cross, built by my grandfather of old railroad ties, was later moved to Long Point. Its small plaque reads:

CHARLES DARBY

GALLANT SOLDIER

KILLED IN ACTION

OCTOBER 17, 1944

Provincetown has never forgotten him.

☞ At Long Point, I might read the paper or walk along the water's edge. There was little use in trying to explore the interior, behind the dune face. Although only yards from the water's edge, the sand became hellishly hot and repelling by midday and stayed that way all afternoon. Usually I would spread my towel on the beach and let the warmth blanket me, inducing a pleasant languor. I rarely gave over completely to sleep, always aware of gulls sweeping over the harbor, of silvery terns hovering, squeaking, and freefalling into a school of feed fish. Aware of the approaching or receding tide, of footsteps crunching the sand, of the buzz of the ancient yellow sightseeing plane overhead, the fragrant sand roses, the muffled sounds of motorboats, the wind boxing the compass. I would stay at the Point until five, maybe six. Sometimes a mist would ride in, a diaphanous curtain that extinguished the sun, left it a pallid wafer, then spread across the harbor. I would watch as the Pilgrim Monument became enshrouded, knowing that it was my bearing home and, if it were totally obscured, I would become lost. With the mist would come a clammy coolness and a pungent brininess that flowed through me, gave me goose bumps, and stood my finest hairs on end. The wind would ruffle the harbor — nothing too ferocious, just enough chop to make the voyage home exhilarating. My small boat would skip across the crests of waves, slapping down into a trough and throwing up a faceful of water. I would feel the sting in my eyes as spindrift dripped off my brow, taste the salt as it rolled over the curve of my lips.

Most afternoons, though, finished quiet and calm, the voluptuous sun perched above the horizon. It was then, and only then, after the sand had cooled, that I could explore the spine of Long Point, rutted by marauding four-wheel-drive vehicles — which are no longer permitted — its oases of sand floating in thickets of stunted, prickly, stubby vegetation.

One afternoon I set out to find a seagull graveyard that Steve at Sal's had once told me about. A friend had told him, though Steve had never seen the place for himself. Following his directions, I began my exploration. He had said to walk down the spine of Long Point from the lighthouse through a patch of lichens and stunted pines to a clearing, a circular flat of sand baked hard by the sun. I easily found the spot, a mysterious place strewn with feathers, hundreds, thousands of odd bones picked clean and bleached, and one or two fresh corpses. Yet outside of this loosely drawn circular boundary, maybe thirty-five feet across, there was not a bone to be found. When my presence became known — and it did almost immediately —

a melee erupted from a raucous passage of gulls overhead. The birds swooped, screamed, dove, and darted, then paused, floating, circling, before again swooping, screaming, diving, darting. I felt that I had intruded into someplace sacred, disturbed the dead. The shadows of the birds overhead swirled over the bones, like souls stirring from the grave. I did not linger and made my way back to the beach.

It always seemed unforgivable to leave Long Point just as evening approached. The landscape was never more handsome, more hypnotic. The late sun softened the rough edges of the jetty, turned the harbor surface opalescent, bathed the beach grass whose limber shadows danced on the cooling dunes. Peeps scurried at the water's edge, dodging the swash, their tiny footprints stitching together the grains of sand, their beaks stabbing the flats in search of worms, sand shrimp, and amphipods.

Even in this pleasure, when the appeal of Long Point was strongest, I didn't give in to its magic. The spell could be broken by a glance across the harbor to that place where the masses mingled, where life was affirmed for me. I was drawn back by thoughts of the evening ahead. Until the quiet had as much to say to me as the music, I couldn't resist the lure of the downtown after sunset.

I would gather up my few belongings for the voyage home, a zigzagging course that took me first to Town Wharf, where the heavy-sitting, rust-streaked draggers, tied four deep broadside, were being picked clean by gulls. The *Hindu* would be readying passengers for a sunset sail, the canopied *Cee Jay* for a narrated tour, the speedboat for its next loop around the harbor. Like seals at an aquarium, a handful of town kids, blue-lipped, teeth chattering, would buoy themselves in the water and wait for quarters, dimes, and nickels to be tossed by spectators. A crowd would gather to watch a tuna weigh-in, the proud fisherman posing for pictures; pickup trucks reeking of fish would cut a swath through a parade of tourists along the wharf. Fishing-party boats and overnight visitors arriving by water would shuttle in and out of boat slips slick with gasoline rainbows. Across the bay, the Truro and Wellfleet shores would come into sharp focus. In the tranquillity of Long Point that my boat and I had left behind, what Byron called the cooling hour — still my favorite time of the day — the caw of gulls and screech of terns would reverberate from one lighthouse to the other.

There was one night, and only one night, when I experienced the serenity of Long Point after dark. Driving around with Crayne, we stopped at New Beach as we did every night, but found ourselves slipping into the tire ruts of vehicles that had gone before us and making our way out onto the beach. We had not planned to flee the din of downtown, but there we were, in what seemed an uncharacteristic act of defiance (or moral strength!) for both of us, under a blackness spangled by a cantering Pegasus, the great winged horse, and by the summer triangle, Vega, Altair, and Deneb. Although I could not see the water line, its presence was betrayed by the breaking surf. The flashing Wood End Light was in front of us; behind, Race Point Light. The air was ripe with salt marsh. The ruts took us up from the beach, into the interior of Long Point and, finally, out to the beach again on the harbor side.

At the Point, the tide was up, the harbor flat and dark. The opposite shoreline reflected the hundreds of colored lights, and the town seemed to rise up out of this watery palette. The distant music, loud and orgiastic in the streets of the town, had become mellifluous by the time it drifted across to Long Point, harmonizing with the gentle breaking of wavelets on the shore and the rush of gull wings, the birds startled and confused by our presence. A boat, a ghost ship with a single light atop its mast, skimmed past, outward bound, making an early start for the fishing grounds, leaving a wake of cool white fire — phosphorescence — in the water. The beacons in the lighthouses' towers, green at Long Point, red at Wood End, danced a pas de deux throughout the night.

We had not intended to stay out on the Point for long, certainly not overnight. We lingered, splashed at the edge of the black sea, tossing handfuls of liquid light into the air. We built a tiny driftwood fire in the sand, talked in whispers, and fell asleep.

Within a few hours the edge of day began trickling out of the east, over Truro. The beach, the dunes, and the harbor were washed in mauve. It is a different experience altogether to witness the dawn from Long Point rather than from a town's bedroom window. By the time the day feeds into the narrow streets, the sun has already cleared the horizon, the light is white. The symphony of daybreak is in its second movement. But from Long Point, the sun rises out of a thread of sand, out of the overture.

The sun on that morning rose in a crescendo, spreading light and heat in every direction. The harbor shone like a spectacular solitaire diamond, the spiraling Provincetown shoreline its gold setting. Overnight, the tide had remade the beach, scrubbing it clean. Trackless, it met the harbor in a gently cusping shoreline. Across the harbor, the town was stirring. Shop doors were flung open, sidewalks hosed down, window boxes watered, awnings unrolled, streets swept, trash picked up, ice chests filled, kegs delivered. We made our way back to town, retracing our route of a few hours earlier. Crayne dropped me at my door and ten minutes later I was on my bike, on my way to work, feeling more alive and restored than if I had slept soundly through the night.

As I did every morning, I rode down to the end of MacMillan Wharf to watch the Portuguese fishermen readying their boats for the trip to Georges Bank. Along with their seafaring tradition, the Portuguese brought to Cape Cod their color, customs, Catholicism, and cuisine, and ultimately the grand celebration of their calling — the annual Blessing of the Fleet.

⑥ Celebrated the last Sunday in June, the Blessing of the Fleet has been a Provincetown spectacle since 1948, a reminder of the livelihood that once sustained Provincetown. There are days of preparation before the big event, vessels hauled out and given new bottom paint; masts, crosstrees, pilothouses, and decks are spruced up with fiery reds, deep blues, hot yellows, and leaf greens. Colored pennants and streamers run up shrouds and stays and snap in the breeze. The hard work of fishing is suspended, and an excitement pervades the town as families coordinate their activities.

During one of my last summers in Provincetown, on Blessing Sunday, I rode my bike along a Commercial Street crisscrossed with bright orange silkscreened pennants but empty of traffic and pageant, rode to the eastern edge of town, swallowing draughts of the new morning, rode back through town and out onto the wharf. Families had begun to arrive, handing foodstuffs and bottles down to husbands, fathers, and sons on boats, who in turn passed the supplies over to the next boat. The boats were scrubbed clean, and the fishy odor that usually permeated the air around MacMillan Wharf was barely detectable. Portuguese, which I rarely heard, tumbled from the tongues of the older generation, whose broad, hearty gestures needed no translator.

Out on Commercial Street the flow of tourists into downtown thickened. Local families made their way in procession from the end of the wharf to St. Peter's for a high mass of thanksgiving co-celebrated by Bishop Cronin and the local clergy. An uncharacteristic solemnity overcame the marchers in remembrance of those now in Neptune's care.

The church doors were thrown open to let in the glory of this early-summer late morning. The pews were full. I sat on my bike, draped over the handlebar, the sun beating down on my back, craning my neck to see in. After mass, families walked down the hill, following a statue of St. Peter, the fisherman's patron saint, carried aloft back to the wharf, where the bishop, on the reviewing stand that became his altar, prepared to give each boat God's blessing for a safe and profitable year.

I broke away from the crowd, pedaling my fastest to the west end, where I retrieved my boat from its mooring and zipped across the harbor. Festooned draggers and trawlers clustered at the end of the wharf — *Gerta Riva, Jimmy Boy, Liberty Belle, Alice J, Victory II, Cap'n Bill, Patricia Marie.* Crowded to their gunwales with generations of families, friends, maybe even a lucky stranger who had endeared him or herself to a boat's owner, each waited to sail past the bishop for anointment. Afterward, they swung their bows around and steamed out to Long Point to link up in the cove for an open-air party.

Following the blessing of the commercial boats, all the other boats were invited to the altar. I took my place in line, with dinghies, Sunfish, canoes, and sport fishers towing rubber rafts, and received the holy water for my little vessel. Rendezvousing with friends, who were in their own boats, our flotilla made its way to the Point. There we joined the bacchanalia, invited to share *cozinha*, lobsters, corn on the cob, grilled linguica, kale soup, fava beans, stuffed quahogs, pork chops soaked in *vinha d'alhos* — a spice-and-garlic marinade — sweet potato–filled turnovers called *trutas*, fisherman's stew, sweet bread — and plenty of drink.

A succulent late light drenched Long Point and the harbor, while a tickling breeze chased away the heat of the afternoon. My shoulders, scalp, and forehead and the back of my legs were frozen with sunburn, my hair dry like tinder, my thoughts clouded by overindulgence, my body exhausted by lack of sleep. At dusk I headed in, the single naked light bulb at the West End Racing Club my beacon, the din of the revelers trailing me across the harbor. Unable to find my mooring, I tossed my anchor over a short distance from shore and made certain that it had grabbed the bottom. I dived into the dark water, blinded, deafened except for the thumping of blood in my skull, feeling my hands stub against the bottom, feeling my skin and scalp absorb the coolness as I swam underwater, surfacing a few feet from the beach. Across the harbor, a wall of fishing boats bearing families cradled in the bent arm of Long Point were rocked ever so gently by the lilt of the sea. A slivered moon reclined in the sky, a hook to hang a prayer on. Tomorrow the boats would return to sea — alone, vulnerable, and in a sea that might not be so friendly.

Summer Ends Now

I LIVED ALONE my last summer in Provincetown. My parents had chosen not to return. After decades of attachment, they had quit Provincetown. Provincetown had become unrecognizable to my parents. Most of the reasons to continue vacationing there had been taken away. There were no family ties. My grandmother was gone. Important artistic expression had found new places to root and flourish, and Provincetown's heyday as an influential art community had come and gone. What had been an ethos of tolerance had deteriorated to license and lawlessness. The remnants of gentility, those last vestiges of convention that held the world together, were derided as square and so very unprogressive.

Among my parents' circle of friends, whose children were our friends, it had become fashionable to encourage, indeed to live vicariously, through their young teenagers' emerging sexuality, to indulge and facilitate their alcohol and drug experimentation, to condone their rebellion as emerging "individuality," to give them their privacy and their "space." Despite what appeared to many, especially our neighbors back home, to be a "liberal," bohemian lifestyle, my parents were conservative and conventional at heart, especially when it came to our upbringing. They knew something about that most pernicious of enemies, unrestrained freedom, and they were unwilling to take their chances with my youngest brother, Matt, then nineteen, now that he was out in the world and out of their

sight. My brother John, preoccupied with a summer base-
ball league back home, had lost interest in Provincetown.
I, too, would not have returned to Provincetown that last
summer except that there were few jobs back home that
would have paid me what I could make in Provincetown.
My parents had made it clear to me, though, that this was
the last of Provincetown.

My digs that last summer were in a bottom apartment
in a converted garage at 5 1/2 Masonic Place, owned by
Halcyone Hurst, Crayne's mother. Because of our friendship she gave me a break on the rent — $900 for the sum-
mer — that enabled me to save something for college and
still have plenty of fun. Though the savings from a summer waitressing job today would hardly pay for more than
books and supplies, back in 1977 the $2,000 that I arrived
home with actually defrayed a good portion of my college
tuition.

At Masonic Place I floated in a thick, cloying attar that
wafted over from across the street from the A-House, vi-
brated to the heavy pulse of disco music from the A-House,
and witnessed foreplay between bronzed boys interlocked
on my doorstep late at night. But like Sal's, and the West
End Racing Club, as far as I was concerned, my little corner
of Provincetown was the center of the universe.

I was surrounded by Mrs. Hurst's family. Her brother,
Reggie Cabral, owned the A-House. Her son FJ and his
wife, Maureen, lived upstairs with their two little girls.
Her daughter Halcyone lived next door with her husband,
Mike, and their two boys. Their kindness toward me over
the years is something I've never forgotten. The seemingly ordinary times when I felt part of the family are the
times that I remember best: watching a Red Sox game
with Crayne's dad at their east-end home; sitting on the
porch on a sultry August night with Crayne's mother; try-

ing Portuguese kale soup for the "first" time at a family dinner; playing with the kids at Masonic Place. I was always greeted with a smile and a "Hello, darling" and accepted by every member of the extended family.

Unlike so many things in life that end before we can make our peace, express our gratitude, or say our proper good-byes, I knew even before I got to town that summer that my wonderful childhood adventure would end on Labor Day. The following summer, after having graduated from college, I would be expected to have a real job and begin my life's work, though I didn't have a clue as to what that work would be.

My future reality tormented me all summer, finding its way into my happiest moments. I wanted to be everywhere at once, with everyone at once, gathering in old friends and new, juggling their attentions, devouring their affections. For days at a time I could not sleep, existing in a state of inquietude, riding my bike out to Race Point, then back to Truro, trying to consume the place. I carried my Instamatic camera with me everywhere, hoping that by making images of slivers of time I might possess the place. I roamed around town night after night, long after everyone had dispersed from Spiritus Pizza, not wanting to go back to the apartment, not wanting the day to end. The next day might not measure up.

☞ I worked that summer at the farthest end of town, waitressing at the Howard Johnson's. I had eagerly anticipated my return to Poyant's, but my job had been given to Russell's younger sister through a behind-the-scenes maneuver that nearly destroyed my cherished friendship with Russell. He confronted his mother and grandmother, who admitted their involvement. I believed him, though, when he said that he knew nothing of the female plot.

But the job change turned out to be fortuitous. I liked HoJo's, made great money and good friends, adding further to my circle of friends that now reached out among townies, the Red Inn boys, and summer residents. I worked the breakfast shift six mornings a week, but as I usually didn't go to bed until 4 A.M., it was not always easy getting myself together for work. I relished my midweek day off, especially if it was rainy or overcast because I could loll in bed until long past lunch without feeling as though I was missing the day. If a rainy day coincided with my day off, I'd spend some of the afternoon downtown at Poor Richard's Buttery eating strawberry muffins, reading, and drinking cup after cup of coffee. Surrounded by walls and furniture painted in the colorful Pennsylvania Dutch folk-art style inspired by Peter Hunt, who had poularized it in the 1940s, I was oblivious to the nasty weather. After Poor Richard's, I'd visited Marine Special-ties and the Rainbow Gallery. After that, there was no design to the day. It unfolded as most days in Provincetown did, on its own terms, each day an improvisation.

On workdays, I'd manage to roust myself from bed after little sleep to take off on my two-mile bike ride along an awakening Commercial Street. Hensche students would be just setting up their easels on the sidewalks, anticipating a few hours of serene morning light. To the casual observer, their habits would have seemed peculiar. They would squint their eyes, repeatedly step up to and then back from their canvases, shake their splayed fingers before their eyes, and put index finger to thumb to create a little frame they'd use to compose their pictures. But I had grown up with such odd behavior and knew exactly what the point of it was.

Except for being confined indoors as these glorious summer days unfolded, I enjoyed my job. We had a good crew. A few older gay men — one most endearing man who called me, affectionately, lovey — one or two older local women, a handful of single guys, my age, in town for the summer, and an equal number of young women, a few years older than I, who had just spent their first winter in Provincetown working at their art or trying to shed memories of bad relationships or stressful jobs.

After a busy breakfast shift, I usually worked the front fountain, scooping ice cream, making sundaes and frappes, perfuming the air with vanilla. At three, I'd be back on my bike, racing home to strip off my uniform and throw on my bathing suit. I didn't waste a minute, pedaling through traffic and tourists to the west end, past all of my old memories, to retrieve my boat. Usually I headed straight to Long Point for my respite. There were afternoons, though, when I stayed on my bike and just kept going to the bike paths in the dunes, or to the woods where Crayne first had taken me to the blind he'd used for winter hunting.

⑥ In its stillness, the woods behind Provincetown, behind the dunes, seemed a place of permanence, of certainties. No ebbing and flowing of harbor, ocean, downtown. No scrubbing clean and being remade each day as was the beach. A twig snapped underfoot this day would be there for tomorrow's walk. A curly shelf fungi would mark the way tomorrow as it did today. A path scored by my feet dragging through pine needles, still there tomorrow. A moldering tree, reclining where it once stood, a signpost. In fact, however, nothing there was truly permanent. Like the beach, the forest was remaking itself, only more slowly.

Wherever there was sunlight, the imperturbable pitch pine stood, pruned by wind and salt spray, often draped in bull briar. For whatever reasons, most of the locals I knew disliked pitch pine in the same way suburbanites did the dandelion. Familiarity, I supposed, bred contempt, even though these resilient trees were binding and stabilizing the very sands upon which the locals stood. Next to sturdy oaks and silky-skinned beech, the pitch pine did seem a bit ungraceful, but I had a special affection for its eccentric posture, dark cracked bark, three-needle bundles, and squat cones, botanical motifs that, more than any others, identified this woods as Cape Cod's.

I never worried that I might get lost in the woods. Lose myself, yes. Get lost, no. I relied upon some primitive instinct that would eventually help me find my way out. It helped that no matter what direction I traveled, I was never very far from the beach or the highway. I always hoped that I would find my way out before dark when the night creatures would venture out with thousands of shiny eyes and ravenous appetites. I feared small, furry, quadrupeds more than I did two-footed strangers.

I'd pedal through the vibrating air of the bike trail, through the corrugated metal tunnel in which I'd yell to hear the echo. When I reached a special spot, I'd stash my bike and plunge into the pathless woods, thick with interlocking branches and leaves, a natural balcony from which birds carried on in clamorous conversation with one another, some in plaintive notes, others gregarious, still others threatening, their nests hidden high in the clutch of branches. Stepping over exposed roots, sidestepping ridges of velvety moss and crunchy reindeer moss and British soldiers, and breathing an air heavy with resins and rot, hormones, and humus, I'd part the cat briar and enter a tabernacle where nature stored her gifts of trillium, Indian pipes, goldenrods, mushrooms, ferns, lilies-of-the-valley, starflowers, lichens, and blueberries. That no one had been there before me, at least not recently, was irresistible. Much of the life of the summer woods was inaccessible, hidden or camouflaged, nature's way, perhaps, of fine-tuning the ear. Clicks. Snaps. Rustlings. Buzzes. Belches. Whinings. Whistles.

I could identify very little of what I saw on my bike rides through the dunes or what I heard and smelled in the woods. Frustrated, I bought a couple of little finder books and Golden Guides for birds and trees and ponds and weeds. Certain that my experience in the woods would be greatly enhanced by a better understanding of dendrology, entomology, limnology, and botany, I would make my way through the vegetation to one of the small ponds hidden off the Beech Forest trail. Provincetown's ponds — unlike the kettle ponds found elsewhere on Cape Cod that were formed from melting chunks of glacial ice — are wind-scoured hollows intersecting the fresh-water table. There, at pondside, I would study the books.

Not long after I began this methodical study of birds and flora, it dawned on me that something was missing. By working so hard at studying, I had ceased to enjoy the spot as much as I had when I couldn't identify my sur-roundings. Distracted, I didn't hear insects vibrating, didn't smell the arresting sweetness of the swamp azalea, ignored the slight summer breeze wrapping around the back of my neck, didn't take in the tiny licks of amber sun-light on the pond surface or the heron shooting out of the rush and grasses and sedges. I realized that I didn't need to have the answers to everything. I could enjoy a breaking wave without knowing its mathematical principle. Enjoy a lunar eclipse without knowing its celestial reasons. Skip stones across the water without knowing why they skip.

From then on, the books stayed behind, on my bureau, sandwiched between a couple of bricks that I had brought back from Long Point, sea-softened artifacts from the old water cisterns. I rediscovered the sheer pleasure of sitting at a pond's edge rimmed with cat-o'-nine-tails that looked liked ceremonial torches and watching the consequence of sending a small pebble airborne on a trajectory that landed it several yards offshore with a throaty splash. Or watching a swarm of monarch butterflies bouncing along on the air. Or a turtle sunning itself on a half-submerged log. Or dragonflies bowing the tips of pond grasses in a graceful curtsy. Or feeling the pulses of pond water, littered with pine needles.

On one of my visits it occurred to me, looking across the creamy, opaque green pool of quiet, that the life of the pond was largely beyond my direct experience. Although I could not see the activity, I knew there was abundance below the surface; producers, consumers, and decomposers; larvae and amphibian metamorphosis; oxygen and carbon dioxide passed back and forth; water molecules bonding their hydrogens together in a tight, elastic surface film. Everything knotted together, exquisitely balanced.

But what appeared to be permanent, certain, really was not. There at pondside the underpinnings were sand, the same ever-vagrant sand of the dunes and the Great Beach. In the woods, as in the dunes and on the beach, there was an ongoing struggle for dominance. As Thoreau had noted, sand had always been the great enemy. In places, it had collected, like a storm front, preparing to slide over and rain down on the forest with its leading edge. In other places, the storm had already passed and the woods had emerged, denuded and vanquished, from the trailing edge. Everywhere else, the forest was still buried.

I knew from my high-school biology class that these ponds were temporary, that in time they would be filled by decomposing vegetation and transformed into marsh or bog, then dry land. Shrubs would take root, then forest growth, first pine, then oak, and ultimately beech. It was a slow process that would take my lifetime, perhaps longer, to complete. I would return here someday, I thought, and not recognize the place.

In nature, we accept that one community will succeed another. The pitch pine survives as long as it receives sunlight, nourishment. Deprived, the pine is taken over by the next generation of forest growth that, in turn, will be taken over by the next. In nature, every step is useful, necessary, incorporating the previous, contributing to the next. We can learn from nature's succession if we remember that its lessons are our lessons.

In contrast to the beach where I wandered aimlessly and collected specimens, I sat in one spot in the woods and let my eyes do the wandering and collecting. After so much time spent by the ocean, it felt odd to be near water but not to hear it. From the pond's shoreline I could see gangly-legged water striders skimming and skating and scavenging. Shiny button-shaped whirligigs, half-submerged, spun giddily across the pond, skating around blue-violet pickerelweed spikes and showy white blossoms of water lilies that rested like teacups on their lily-pad saucers where damselflies touched down. Green frogs, croaking like banjos, poked their faces through a surface flowing with algae mats. Unseen bullfrogs belched their jug-o'-rum harmonies. Fowler toads rustled the friable leaves next to me. I poked the leaves with a stick and watched as the tiny pale creatures hopped away. I had no interest in catching one, taking seriously the admonitions heard during childhood about toads and warts. I dodged swarming, bulbous-eyed, turquoise dragonflies and was careful not to wade too far out into the pond for fear that leeches would attach themselves to my legs. I was reminded of those myths from childhood that connected me to every other kid who had heard them: that dragonflies would "darn" your lips together and that leeches would inject their anticoagulant called hirudin and drain your blood. Despite my growing knowledge of the natural world, I had never found anything in the books that said such things didn't happen. I still wonder if bats do, in fact, like to tangle in hair.

Thick air hung over the woods. Slants of light that slipped in through the trees backlighted spiderwebs strung between branches and illuminated clouds of no-see-ums and mosquitoes. It was time to leave the forest's shadows and secrets, but not before stopping for a handful of blueberries.

One late afternoon I emerged from the woods and cut through the cemetery on my way back into town. It was a part of Provincetown, behind the congestion of downtown, that I had never really explored — but that day, for reasons I still do not understand, a vague memory was stirred of a visit there years earlier. We had been leaving town and my mother had pulled the car in. She had said that my grandfather's grave was there and then had commented on the cemetery's lack of upkeep.

I walked my bike in among the headstones and started reading names and dates, intrigued equally by the octogenarians and those who had not survived infancy. A rotund, tank-topped man trimming around the headstones asked me if I needed help in locating a grave. After saying no, I changed my mind and told him that my grandparents were John and Vivienne Whorf. I asked if he might know where their graves were. Not only did he point me in the right direction, but he told me precisely where the headstone was.

I pedaled back up the hill and approached a spot tucked behind a screen of cedars and off by itself in a far corner

of the cemetery. I expected to find the grave still un-
kempt, although the cemetery seemed to be generally well
maintained. The area, with just a few graves, had been
tended to, the wildflowers and weeds cut back. Under the
searing summer sun, the groundcover was thinly stub-
bled, dry and brittle in the sandy soil. I had imagined that
my grandparents would have selected some artsy headstone and was unprepared when I looked up and saw their
names chiseled in block letters in a chunk of brown stone,
polished front and back, rough around its edges:

JOHN WHORF 1903–1959
VIVIENNE WHORF 1903–1972

On the reverse side of the headstone, simply WHORF.
Nothing to say who they were or how they lived. Nothing
heroic like the inscriptions for those lost at sea. Nothing
poignant like, "Our Angel" or "Beloved" or "Friend to All."
Not even "Mother" or "Father." Nothing.

My grandmother had died in a house fire only five
years earlier, though I could not remember what she had
looked like. My brothers and I did not go her funeral; my
parents were down and back before we got home from
school that day. I never had the chance to say good-bye,
the first time death had touched my life.

That late afternoon in the cemetery, I felt I had been
summoned for a reason, as we are summoned on a few occasions during our life, to be helped across a divide, to be
offered a moment of recognition, of apprehension. The
timing was right to receive that moment. Although I had
been saying good-bye to Provincetown all summer, it was
only while sitting there in the cemetery, staring at my
grandparents' headstone, that I fully understood good-
bye. I promised myself that day that I would not squander

one minute of those last days of summer, one minute of the life I had been given.

℘ There was always, in those dwindling days of summer, a moment when the night air carried a hint of autumn, faint and plaintive, like a bagpiper's tune heard in the distance. With that moment came something more elusive, a hint of sadness and vague despair that went beyond summer's ending. Sunlight became tinged with amber; plants surrendered their lush greens; the beach grass sprouted seed plumes; the glasswort colored the marsh in hues of red; shorebirds massed for their journey along the flyway. In the harbor, boats were reduced to the few that belonged to locals that would stay put until the first frost. Having visited my grandmother every Christmas when she was alive, I knew what the off-season held. Dead streets. Empty harbor. Chill. Boarded windows. A midnight darkness by late afternoon. The town buried in snow as it had been in sunlight not so many weeks earlier. A Hopper melancholy.

Summer after summer, throughout my childhood and teens, I had prayed that something would delay our departure — car trouble, an unexpected arrival on Sal's patio, some old face from the past for whom my parents were willing to linger a little longer, an act of God. One Labor Day weekend, with the car packed and my parents ready, God had complied, sending a tropical storm whose winds and sheeting rain closed the Sagamore Bridge up-Cape.

In Provincetown, the storm frothed up the harbor, rippled the soaked streets, stood the Stars and Stripes straight out from the flag poles, tore leaves from branches and matted them onto windows and screens. There was a flurry of movement out in the harbor to secure boats, and we could see that one had broken from its mooring and was slamming against the pilings of the cold-storage wharf that was also being battered by the sea. We drove out to Race Point where a crowd had gathered to see crashing, furious water throw its anger high up onto the beach and the beach hurl its sand right back.

Returning to the west end, we splashed at the water's edge with our legs, blasted by the sand, dangling out of yellow raincoats. Depending on which way we were walking, we were either shoved along by the wind or we pushed against it, gulping it, hoping to make headway.

By late afternoon, though the furious weather had not subsided in Provincetown, it had abated enough up-Cape to reopen the bridge. The inevitable had only been delayed. Once again, I was saying good-bye, promising to stay in touch, to write, to call, until, once again, I would be sitting on the beach, digging and pushing at the coarse sand with my hands and feet, letting the glassy white grains of quartz, the gray feldspar, the reddish garnet slip through my fingers and toes.

In the early years, after saying good-bye to the O'Donnells and the folks at Sal's, we would stop at the Provincetown Inn, where my grandmother worked in the gift shop. My brothers and I would spin the postcard racks, chase each other with stuffed, velvety lobsters, and sample the soap and candle fragrances while my parents said their good-byes. As a parting gesture, my grandmother would invite me to choose from a shelf full of little wooden dolls dressed in international costumes. I still have those little dolls.

From the Provincetown Inn we'd curl around the salt marsh and onto the highway. Across East Harbor, into Truro. I was tucked in the back of the station wagon, facing backward, watching Provincetown recede, unwilling to let go of summer until I absolutely had to, until I could no longer see the monument, clinging to the only place, the only time, when everything was good. Back then, though, Provincetown emptied like a busted levee and it helped, somewhat, to assuage my sense of loss knowing that everyone else was leaving at the same time I was.

It was not the town and the landscape that I missed then as much as I did the people who had shared my summer life. When I was younger, little seemed to change summer to summer, but as I grew older, I became aware of the tidal quality of life, people coming in, going out, then new people coming in, only to recede, too. All those good-byes at Sal's, behind the Racing Club, at Race Point, or at the Red Inn were not only good-byes to summer, but goodbyes to an irretrievable oneness with another person, some deeply realized human need. Try as I might to accumulate everything and everyone, it was not possible to carry it all, not only because of the sheer load, but because every relationship depended on a precise confluence of time and place for its potency. New relationships pushed the old ones further and further into memory.

⑥ As I drove home for the last time that last summer, I piled every other summer, every corner of Provincetown, every person, every hour, into a bundle of tender memories. My childhood flickered. I turned left onto High Head Road and drove up to Pilgrim Heights, a balcony that looked out over the dollhouse cottages at Beach Point, out across the bay to the lonely, steady green light at Long Point, and to Provincetown, which — to use Edna St. Vincent Millay's words — was "my shining palace built upon the sand." The monument was illuminated, and I looked one last time on its shapes and shadows in which we all could see Donald Duck's face.

I passed the turn for the Pamet roads. I remembered the Pamet dances of my later teen years when we rode out of P-Town on the tailgate of Ronny's pickup. Those dances were like every other childhood dance: girls on one side, boys on the other. I couldn't remember ever having been asked to dance, but I had had a great time nonetheless, doing what, I can't remember. A great time doing nothing. Just being. Thoreau knew the pleasure.

"I am grateful for what I am and have," he wrote. "My thanksgiving is perpetual. It is surprising how contented one can be with nothing definite — only a sense of existence. My breath is sweet to me. Oh, how I laugh when I think of my vague indefinite riches. No run on my bank can drain it for my wealth is not possession but enjoyment."

At the bend in Route 6, in Wellfleet, I was ambushed again by the rich odor of the salt marsh. Across the marsh was Great Island in Wellfleet, and I remembered a night that I had lain in the bow of the eroding dune, drinking too much wine and watching the sunset with Will, a friend from Howard Johnson's. We could see a tiny Pilgrim Monument out there on the horizon.

Nauset Beach. Mayo's Farm. I passed the Cape Cod Coliseum at mid-Cape and remembered Chuck Berry and Three Dog Night concerts with Larry, Timmy, and Ricky. I was so absorbed in thought that I nearly missed my exit off Route 3 an hour later. I turned off and passed through the intersection and onto Main Street in Hing-ham, dark and canopied by elms and maples. Everything looked fresh and new there, where I lived nine months of the year. The crickets and cicadas and katydids were in full throat, as they were every September upon my return, a last rousing refrain before the curtain dropped on summer.

They were singing in the Provincetown woods, too, and all the shiny eyes were open. In the west end, the last dinners were being served at Sal's. Downtown, the last Chablis was being sipped at galleries. At Piggies, last call. Soon the locals would reclaim their town. They would eagerly await hunting season and fish the outer beach again without encountering a fleet of out-of-state RVs. The town boys would start trying to woo back their old girl-friends who they had so cavalierly dumped when the summer girls had arrived. There would be ice-boating on East Harbor. Flipper breakfasts. PTO. VFW. Town meeting. School sports. Rug-hooking classes. Holidays would bring together long-unseen family members.

Late that September night, in the quiet of my bedroom, after everyone else was asleep, I spread my keepsakes all over the bed, as I had done every summer, and then looked to my giant bulletin board to see where I might make space for some of it. This odd assortment — beer-bottle labels, movie-ticket stubs, cocktail napkins, shells, stones, matchbooks, restaurant receipts, a pressed flower, a cellophane packet of sand, a seagull feather — was stuff I collected every year. Inscribed with date and place, each was like a piece of the road map I used to renavigate the summers.

There was a note from Russell that he had tacked to my apartment door. "We're over at the A-House. Come over. Russell." And one from Billy: "I'll be up in my room reading if you want to stop by. Billy." I sorted through the packages of photographs that I had mailed home from Province-town; they came back to me as moments as real and as viscerally potent as when I had first experienced them.

While I sifted through my keepsakes, the transistor radio played songs in tribute to Elvis, who had died too soon, too young, a few weeks earlier. When I'd heard about it, I had been in my Provincetown apartment, tossing a basketball with a friend, preparing to go out in the boat. Instead, we had sat down on the beds, sunlight pouring in through the open front door, and listened to the songs. Alone in my room in Hingham, I did the same. Elvis's smoky, mellow voice, the sweet, wild songs of his youth — youth that takes so much for granted, especially time — eventually sang me to sleep.

When I awoke the next morning, my keepsakes were still strewn on the bed, reminders of all that I had left behind. Were it not for those tangible reminders, I might have thought I had dreamed it all. It seemed I had been away forever and that I hadn't been away at all. Memories of events were already dimming, and I was full of regret for what I had not done, for the time I had wasted. I could have laughed more, loved more, been kinder, listened more, walked more, danced more, gone to Long Point once more, to the woods, the dunes, the marsh once more, breathed in the rose, the privet, the sand, the salt once more. Done everything more. Once more.

But there would be another day. Provincetown would always be there. Although I'd be working in Boston the following summer, I would go to P-Town for weekends, go to Piggies and Spiritus, slip back in and wear the place like a pair of comfortable Levi's, pick up with everyone, as old friends do, right where we had left off. I'd do everything once more. Not a moment would be squandered. That was the lesson I had learned and the promise I had made to myself, standing at my grandparents' graveside on a late summer afternoon. I'd do everything once more. With passion. I had promised.

Epilogue

NOT LONG AGO, I opened an air freshener and its scent released in me fleeting, vivid memories of the produce truck unloading in front of Sal's and of fruit fermenting in the August heat at Perry's Market. My memories were not always so sweet, but the stream of time has carried away the profound sense of loss that for so long lingered after my affair with Provincetown ended. I have learned there can be love after parting.

After finishing college in May of 1978, I went to work in Boston, the first summer of my life that I was not living in Provincetown. My brother John and I decided rather spontaneously one Friday morning that we would drive to P-Town for the weekend. It was in many ways a sentimental journey for me. Along Route 6, the past came back to me, and I felt again as though I was tucked in the back of the old Falcon wagon. We passed all the familiar signposts — the Wellfleet Drive-in, the salt marsh, the clay cliffs in Truro. Just as it had been when I was a kid, we couldn't get there fast enough, but finally we arrived in Provincetown on a sweltering Friday evening.

We had planned to stay with Russell, who had returned for another summer. Rather than stay with his grandmother, he had rented a cottage on Bradford Street, too small, it turned out, for everyone who showed up that weekend expecting a bed. I didn't care. I was back in Provincetown, and that was all that mattered. After a night of dancing at Piggie's and eating pizza on the curb at Spiritus, Johnny and I spent what was left of it in the car, parked behind the Community Center. When we awoke around 5:30, we drove to the west end, where a morning swim in the harbor behind the club washed away the effects of the night's restless sleep. Alone there, with no cottage, no job to go to, no real purpose, the realization came to me: I was a vagabond, an interloper, looking in from the outside. After twenty-two summers, how could it have all ended so abruptly, my identity drowned, my place in the universe lost?

Too much of my identity had come from Provincetown. Even when I had left Provincetown that Labor Day weekend the previous summer, knowing that it would be my last as a summer resident, I was sure that Provincetown would continue be a part of me in the way it had always been, that I could go back, that I would always be a part of it. But like a cluster of blue mussels, I had been removed from my habitat, had lost my attachment. What I could not know then was that this ending was also a beginning, that the passing away of one thing to make room for another applied to my life, too.

That morning, that glorious summer morning that was in so many ways no different than any of the hundreds of other summer mornings, I had crossed an invisible Rubicon, leaving behind childhood, letting go of that splendid and blissful state that had endowed Province-town with only halcyon days and Elysian fields.

I had felt protected by my life in Provincetown. There, I never felt vulnerable, never felt judged. Although I was not especially attractive, there I felt pretty because I felt confident, because I belonged. The clannish Portuguese seemed to have forgiven me my father's and grandparent's aloofness and superiority. In Provincetown, my mother's frustrations and unhappiness, her struggle to be acknowl-edged as an accomplished painter had dissolved in the sunny cadmiums of her watercolors. My father's unfulfilled potential, of which he was keenly aware, did not weigh on him as it did in Hingham, an increasingly affluent town where he had the evidence of success all around him. In Provincetown he had an identity — if only as the son of a well-known painter. It occurs to me now that perhaps they, too, had been ripped from a special place where they might have thrived. I did not understand that then, what detachment could do to me or to them, to anyone. All I knew was that in Provincetown, for a few months every year, for twenty-two years, everything had been good. It had been the only place, the only time, when everything had felt good.

From the moment of that morning swim, I never again saw Provincetown in the same way. It was time for me to relinquish the illusions of childhood.

It had been impossible for me to see through the glare of summer's exuberance and extroversion, through the hopeful light of childhood that had invested everything with goodness. Now detached from it all and older, I began to understand that elusive something, that hint of sadness, of vague despair that, as a child, I had always sensed with autumn's approach. It was not merely the letdown of summer's end; it was the bottoming out of the manic happiness that could not be sustained.

In a fit of vengeance and spite, I shunned Provincetown, convinced that I had outgrown the town, a place of whims and ephemeral pleasures, of self-aggrandizement, this place where people, forever escaping, forever searching, ended up because they could go no farther or further. I told myself that I was one of the fortunate who, deaf to its seductive song, had been spared. But I had escaped only physically. Emotionally, the place never left me alone anymore than, long after parting, thoughts of an old love do. The past tormented me with its presence. I tried in every way I knew to annihilate the place from memory. "How natural it is to destroy what we cannot possess, to deny what we do not understand, and to insult what we envy," wrote Balzac. But I could not forget. I could only lament that the kiss and the whisper, so ephemeral in themselves, stayed so sweet and buoyed so long in memory. And I always knew that I would eventually return.

    A decade later I did return, determined to search for those first affections, the love of my childhood for the P-Town that had been lost in my anger and denial. If you lose something, said someone who must have, go back to the last place you had it. What I did not expect to find was that being cast out led to a deeper appreciation and, in time, a new relationship.

The changes in the Provincetown that I returned to in 1988 were pronounced. By the middle of the 1980s, AIDS had settled in, and with the new epidemic came an AIDS culture of political activism and demands for gay health and support services that polarized and politicized the town. The single-issue stridency, and the arrival of infected young men whose only interest in Provincetown was its support network, alienated townies and strained the harmony, the live-and-let-live attitude that had always been the town's philosophy. The carefree, hedonic pursuits of the 1970s were eclipsed by militancy and memorial services. Where once I had been entertained by the "happy" downtown party, now I saw it with a deep pathos, saw it as a human tragedy that so many young men in the prime of lives would spend that life prancing around downtown in reindeer antlers or a diaper or a ballerina's costume.

The plague, which spawned fear, suspicion, and gaunt men, could not have come at a worse time for Provincetown, already uneasy with the degree to which homosexuals were infiltrating the political infrastructure and buying up real estate. It was a classic immigrant scenario, the haves — in my day, the Portuguese — suddenly becoming the have-nots. To further exacerbate the identity crisis, Provincetown — overbuilt, overcondo-ized, and overpriced — was threatened by honky-tonk superficiality, a languishing fishing industry, rising unemployment and poverty, deteriorating water quality, controversial septic and landfill issues, uninspired art, and an exodus by local residents to neighboring Truro. Perhaps most ominous was the dearth of children to give Provincetown a future, a memory.

Time had also brought changes to the old neighborhood. The cold storage, which had fallen in on itself after being abandoned, had been replaced by the Coast Guard station. The trap shed had been razed only days after being nominated for landmark status, and the spindly wharf had been replaced by a concrete pier. Joe Cow had died; the Red Inn had been sold, the boys dispersed around the country. A local had bought Sal's Place and A Home at Last, which he had remodeled and modernized. Although the inside of the cottage had been renovated, the outside looked pretty much as it always had. A few familiar faces and a few artists still lingered about the place, but the children's voices had been silenced.

A condominium now stood on Flyer's little bit of heaven, and Flyer's fleet of orange-and-white dories had been moved, out of view, to the far side of the Coast Guard pier. On the once-lovingly tended open lot next to Perry's, two dwellings overwhelmed the space, completely obstructing the view of the harbor and Long Point. No more freshly cut grass smells, no more toes slipping through the dew-soaked pile, no more full moons rolling out their boardwalk of light across the harbor and up Nickerson Street.

There was still a market where Perry's had been, but there were no fresh fruit fragrances. Everything was refrigerated. The lighthouse at Long Point had been fitted with awkward, slanted solar panels that destroyed its simple symmetry, the quaint silhouette that my camera had captured so many times against a setting sun. Where once there was freedom to roam, there were rules, regulations, requirements, restrictions, bans, quotas, chains, fences, fees, and permits. And signs, everywhere signs: Keep Off. Beware of Dog. Violators Will Be Towed. Do Not Trespass. Do Not Enter. Private Property.

As if by some miracle, the West End Racing Club remained a lone survivor in a sea of change. It looked exactly as it had when I had learned how to rig a Sunfish. Young, hopeful, sun-browned children still scrambled for tillers, centerboards, and sails and bounded down the worn planked steps to the beach where the boats were waiting at water's edge. Inside the clubhouse, the gull and buoy, the monument, and the international flags I had painted all those years before were still there. My "masterpieces" had survived.

So, too, had the salt marsh, the flats, the dunes, the woods of my early memories. I remembered how I had always thrilled in discovering the landscape's sensuousness and gifts — the secret world under a lily pad, the hermit crab changing houses, orangey-red and metallic blue-green clam worms slithering across the flats, starfish on the breakwater, their arms draped casually over one another, thickets of blueberries and colonies of sand dollars. And it was by reacquainting with nature that I gradually excavated the past and built a future.

ⓑ The downtown, once and for so long my raison d'être, holds nothing for me now. I thrill again in discovering the landscape and remembering that glow in my heart, "the feeling that I could last forever," to use Conrad's words. I spy a moon snail plowing across the flats foraging for a shellfish dinner. I pluck him from the shallows and watch as he gathers his foot into his shell, still not believing that it will all fit snugly. It does. Some things never change.

I sit patiently, nibbling on a sea pickle, watching flat floes of sand hitching a ride into the panne-pocked salt marsh on a silent, probing finger of tide. Overhead, a frenzied flock of swallows performs its air show. A leggy green heron pokes around in the wrack, and a tincture of skunk wafts out from the upper marsh. Hay reclines in tousled cowlicks. I cherish them because they remind me of myself as a spirited child, tanned, always barefooted with air-dried, tousled hair cascading down my back.

In the woods, fragrant with a simmering potpourri of fallen leaves, curls of bark, pine needles, berries, and acorn caps, I have discovered a mother lode of blueberries. As I let them tumble off my hand and into my container, I remember another day of blueberrying under a blazing sun. I lie on the small dock that reaches out into one of the ponds choked with vegetation and watch the water striders dimpling the surface as they glide around it. The air is sweetened by fragrant water nymphs. I have come to know the woods in all its seasonal incarnations — the young greens of spring, the blunt fullness and raging passion of summer, the clarity and brilliance of autumn, the dusky grays and cold, blue light of winter.

I launch an inflatable canvas raft on East Harbor and drift out to the silent middle, feeling the wind-ruffled water rolling under me. At dusk, a blue heron takes flight out of the grasses, cattails, and phragmites. Out at New Beach I find a grapefruit-sized sea wash ball — the egg case of the knobbed whelk — and from the same jetty whose shadows once tucked me in, I watch the setting sun streak the sky a light maroon behind Race Point Light and Hatches Harbor. I wonder if such a color can be mixed on an artist's palette. Then I turn my back on the sun and watch the waning light gild the landscape. After darkness falls, I join a Seashore ranger and a small group of out-of-town visitors for a campfire on the beach and remember another campfire licking and snapping at the night. Offshore, a dragger steams home from the Stellwagen, and I remember another fishing boat with a single light atop its mast, skimming past, outward bound.

On a night walk in the dunes we are led by a ranger who, with his long coat, brimmed hat, and walking stick, is an apparition of Thoreau. It is a silent walk. No one speaks for two hours. We stop to see the bowl of a dune glow in the moonless black, to feel the wind swirl in our ears, to hear the ocean — and two lovers who think they are alone. I see Pegasus and I am reminded of another night, out on Long Point, when I saw him flying on his back up into the late summer sky.

I am fulfilled by Long Point. The coming tide sprawls onto the beach and a tongue of water channels into the shallow lobster plain, tickling the sands, eddying, wending its way, relentlessly, as though with some memory of its previous visit, absorbed by the parched sands until the tide retreats, leaving the beach sculpted, transformed.

I shed my clothes and ease into the water, into a swarm of transparent, jewel-like, feeble comb jellies, morphing into oneness with the sea, feeling its coolness fill in and around me, capture me, nourish me with its biological wealth. The salt buoys me and I float, all but my face submerged, in a perfect equilibrium, nudged, rocked, rolled, like the jellies, by the water. I am completely free at that moment. It is what I do with my freedom that is my challenge.

Later, I lie in the sand and let the heat of the grains and the sun's warmth sandwich me. Then I walk, a leisurely, sauntering, slumping, rolling, rubbery kind of walk with no particular plan. My body is dry and I lick the salt from my forearm, a ritual I had outgrown only to have grown into it again. The sun tracks across the sky and hangs over the horizon, repelling night, glinting off the landscape's saffrons and greens, its redness flattened on the bottom as though the dunes were trying to nudge it back up into the sky. Long after the hour when I used to pack up my things and head in, I am still there.

In the space, all that space between the lights, romantic notions roam free. I become a modern-day Crusoe, endowed with strength, imagination, mental resourcefulness, comfortable being alone.

I explore the littoral zone, losing myself and all sense of time, though when I look at my watch it seems time has stood still. I gather opalescent pebbles, skate egg cases, horseshoe crab sheds, moon snails, slipper shells, razors, and drills. I explore the dune swales, trying to decipher the footprints left by small animals, delighting still in the perfection of compass grass circles. I spy brown egg shells, speckled darker, resting on a pillow of dried marsh grass, down feathers and bits of blackened wrack. I notice that a patch of salt marsh has advanced since last year and I smell its ripeness. I hear the outgoing tide draining out of the flats, spattering like a steady, light rain.

I've come to appreciate the strange beauty and grace in nature's grimmest moments. On one walk, I find a gull, prone at the base of Long Point Light, crushed by its impact with the cement wall. Though broken, it lies in a beautiful position, its neck and beak horizontal, its body extending perpendicular with the elbow of one wing gently touching the beak.

Another gull at the water's edge has been eviscerated. As the waves spill over it, pushing it, pulling it, rolling it, it performs a morbid tableau vivant, striking poses and holding them until the next wave. One convulsive wave casts the bird high enough onto the beach that it remains high and dry for a few moments, one wing forming a long, gentle curve reminiscent of the outer beach, its neck, head, and beak whorling in the same way as does Long Point. Occasionally, the tide carries in and deposits something of its own — a bluefish skeleton, a tuna head, or the sand skate whose white underbelly I spot from far down the beach.

There have been lessons learned by all this wandering and watching. I hear and am ever mindful of Hawthorne's words to his student painters to see, as if for the first time, to see each day's individuality of color. We are made young again by seeing as if for the first time, the way children see. We are made young again by discovery, by the possibility, however remote, that we might find something new on the same beach we walked yesterday.

We need to let ourselves be lured to the edge, commit to adventure, to being beachcombers through life. Uninhibited and curious — like children — we may consider and appreciate each thing along the way, saving and cherishing the precious few that speak to us, add to us.

My beachcomber's journal is crowded with events and discoveries, my pail with all sorts of treasures that I bring home and lay out, in no particular order or design, on the top of my computer, on my desk, on the fence in my garden, around my fishpond. One night, I'll be sitting at the computer, my reflection staring back at me, and I'll pick up one of the chalky, dulled specimens and press it to my tongue, and the moisture will bring it back to life, make it glisten, bring back the colors that will remind me why I picked it up off the beach and why it was one of the precious ones I saved.

On every visit to the flats, the salt marsh, the dunes, the woods I am rediscovering those first affections, boxing the compass, returning to a place where virtues are simple, possibilities many, choices fundamental, and the truth is not so hard to find. "There is no fence or hedge around time that has gone," wrote a time-traveling sage. "You can go back and have what you like if you remember it well enough." The journey home has been puddled with vagrant sands and mirages, with debilitating memories of days gone by, with indefinable, sometimes unbearable, longings, with fears, regrets, cruelties, and passions that only ceased to haunt me once I embraced them.

We make the perilous journey back in time to remember, to rediscover the essence of ourselves, to retrieve the spirit that is all too often snuffed out by life and by those around us. When we are called to make the journey, we cannot ignore the call. We need to know where we came from and where we have left.

I wrote my story as a simple portrait of a time and place. I wrote this story to tell about Provincetown and to say that we can, all these years later, surrender ourselves to a song from childhood. We can go back. I can pick up a moon snail shell, press it to my ear, and listen to the eternal music of the sea. I hear the water music forever playing deep inside. In my mind's eye, the tide is up and the sun is beating down.

CODE OF ETHICS

The West End Racing Club, after due thought and consideration of the elements of FAIR PLAY, has adopted the following set of requirements, which shall be deemed a responsibility of every enrollee admitted to the program of the club:

1. To respect the property of others.
2. To treat other people as equals.
3. To play the game properly.
4. To win fairly and squarely.
5. To lose as a gentleman.
6. To help when help is needed.
7. To aid the club as required to preserve its property in an emergency.
8. To compete for fun.
9. To share privileges with others.
10. To do a proper share of the work always.

It is the earnest hope and wish of the Directors of this club that adult direction to a minimum degree will be necessary to achieve the goal of GOOD SPORTSMANSHIP.

Most depends on each young sailor in the group. Each will adopt the CODE, we are sure.

WEST END RACING CLUB